MW00380419

CI Marketing, cimprint@msn.com

ISBN-13: 978-1508801221
ISBN-10: 1508801223

BISAC: REL046000 RELIGION / Christianity / Church of Jesus Christ of Latter-day Saints (Mormon)

The Great Gathering
Table of Contents

Introduction

Introduction - Look for Patterns

This book is a compilation of dreams, visions and near death experiences that have passages concerning the end-times as spoken of in the scriptures, the time just prior to the return of our Savior Jesus Christ. It is also a compilation of scriptures, general authority quotes and other resources rich in detail and sometimes instruction.

My purpose in pulling together a myriad of resources I have gathered over the years to share with others was influenced by Elder Oaks talk in General Conference, April 2004:

> **Elder Oaks** in the April 2004 General Conference encouraged all members of the Church throughout the world to "**accelerate** our own preparation and try to **influence** the preparation of those around us."

When we read them all together in one place, our own mind becomes more focused and we can start to see the patterns, hidden messages, and new insights.

> **Elder Bednar**, in a speech on the 4th of February, 2007 states:
>
> In my judgment, diligently searching to discover connections, _patterns_, and themes is in part what it means to "feast" upon the words of Christ. This approach can open the floodgates of the spiritual reservoir, enlighten our understanding through His Spirit, and produce a depth of gratitude for the holy scriptures and a degree of spiritual commitment that can be received in no other way. Such searching enables us to build upon the rock of our Redeemer and to withstand the winds of wickedness in these latter days.

Patterns in the Scriptures of God Calling Out His People

One pattern in the scriptures is the calling out of the righteous from among the wicked, prior to the destruction of a wicked city or wicked group of people. The Lord never fails to call them out, away from the destruction, so He can protect them.

Here are some patterns of God calling His people out to protect them:

- The first story in the Book of Mormon: Lehi and Nephi were fleeing before the destruction of Jerusalem.
- Noah and his family: The Lord "sealed" the ark to keep those who did not prepare out.
- The Jaredites were led to the promised land.
- Abraham (more than once), before getting into Egypt.
- Lot fled Sodom and Gomorrah.
- Joseph and Mary fled to Egypt.
- Moses took the children of Israel into the wilderness and then on to the promised land.
- The Early Saints fled to Utah to get away from persecution.

General Authority Quotes for a Gathering

Henry B. Eyring - Raise the Bar (BYU-Idaho Talk - January 2005)

"The giant earthquake, and the tsunami it sent crashing into the coasts around the Indian Ocean, is just the beginning and a part of what is to come, terrible as it was.

You remember the words from the Doctrine and Covenants which now seem so accurate: (He quotes D&C 88:88-91)

Fear shall come upon all people. But you and I know that the Lord has <u>prepared places of safety</u> to which he is eager to guide us....It will be our choice whether or not to move up or stay where we are. But the Lord will invite and guide us upward by the direction of the Holy Ghost...."

Elder H. Aldridge (Second Quorum of the Seventy) LDS Business College Devotional, February 8th, 2005

"We must both learn what these signs are and then identify them correctly when they occur. They can and will strengthen our faith in Christ and His prophets, if we know the scriptures. <u>Just as in the days of Noah, a way is already prepared for the escape of the Lord's elect Latter-Day Saints, if they are in tune with His prophets.</u>"

Brigham Young
"An inland Empire will be established in these valleys of the mountains, <u>which will be a place of refuge for millions of people to gather to</u>, when the great day of the judgments of God comes upon the earth, and the righteous come here for safety. Our people will go East..., West, North and South, but the day will come, when they will be glad to come back. We will be shut out from the rest of the world."

5

Joseph Smith The Teachings of the Prophet Joseph Smith, Section 2, P.71

"...for without Zion, _and a place of deliverance_, we must fall; because the time is near when the sun will be darkened, and the moon turn to blood, and the stars fall from the heaven, and the earth reel to and fro.

Then, if this is the case, and _if we are not sanctified and gathered to the places God has appointed,_ with all our former professions and our great love for the Bible, we must fall; we cannot stand; we cannot be saved; for _God will gather out his saints_ from the Gentiles, and then comes desolation and destruction, and none can escape except the pure in heart who are gathered."

Joseph Smith DHC 4:272

"_In addition to all temporal blessings, there is no other way for the Saints to be saved in these last days, than by gathering...._"

Harold B. Lee Conference Report, April 1948

"Thus, clearly, _the Lord has placed the responsibility for directing the work of gathering in the hands of the leaders of the Church to whom he will reveal his will where and when such gatherings would take place in the future._

It would be well before the frightening events concerning the fulfillment of all God's promises and predictions are upon us, that the Saints in every land prepare themselves and _look forward to the instruction that shall come to them from the First Presidency of this Church as to where they shall be gathered_ and not be disturbed in their feelings until such instruction is given to them as it is revealed by the Lord to the proper authority."

President Woodruff asked: "Can you tell me where the people are who will be shielded and protected from these great calamities and judgments which are even now at our doors? I'll tell you. The priesthood of the God who honor their priesthood, and who are worthy of their blessings are the only ones who shall have this safety and protection. They are the only mortal beings. No other people have a right to be shielded from these judgments. _They are at our very doors; not even this people will escape them entirely._ They will come down like the judgments of Sodom and Gomorrah. And none but the priesthood will be safe from their fury." (Young Women's Journal, Aug 1894, P. 512.)

Scriptures Concerning a Gathering

Moses 7:59–62;
"And the day shall come that the earth shall rest, but before that day the heavens shall be darkened, and a veil of darkness shall cover the earth; and the heavens shall shake, and also the earth; and great tribulations shall be among the children of men, but my people will I preserve;
And righteousness will I send down out of heaven; and truth will I send forth out of the earth, to bear testimony of mine Only Begotten; his resurrection from the dead; yea, and also the resurrection of all men; and righteousness and truth will I cause *to sweep the earth as with a flood*". (Our social media missionary work today. We are in the "hastening".)

Revelations 18:4 "Come out of her my people . . . that ye receive not of her plagues." "Come out" in Greek that means "Exodus".

Isaiah 51:3 "For the Lord shall comfort Zion, He will comfort all her waste places; and He will make her wilderness like Eden, and her desert like the garden of the Lord. Joy and gladness shall be found therein, thanksgiving and the voice of melody."

Isaiah 26: 20 Come, my people, enter thou into thy chambers, and shut thy doors about thee: hide thyself as it were for a little moment, until the indignation be overpast.
21 For, behold, the Lord cometh out of His place to punish the inhabitants of the earth for their iniquity: the earth also shall disclose her blood, and shall no more cover her slain.

Rev 3:14 And to the woman were given two wings of a great eagle, that she might fly into the wilderness, into her place, where she is nourished for a time, and times, and half a time, from the face of the serpent.

Alma 26:5-8
"Yea, they shall not be beaten down by the storm at the last day; yea, neither shall they be harrowed up by the whirlwinds; but when the storm cometh they shall be gathered together in their place, that the storm cannot penetrate to them; yea, neither shall they be driven with fierce winds whithersoever the enemy listeth to carry them. But behold, they are in the hands of the Lord of the harvest, and they are his; and He will raise them up at the last day. Blessed be the name of our God; let us sing to His praise, yea, let us give thanks to His holy name, for He doth work righteousness forever."

Are we getting close to a time of gathering?

President Ezra Taft Benson, March 4, 1979

"For nearly six thousand years, God has held you in reserve to make your appearance in the final days before the Second Coming of the Lord...God has saved for the final inning some of His strongest and most valiant children, who will help bear off the kingdom triumphantly. That is where you come in, for you are the generation that must be prepared to meet your God."

President Gordon B. Hinckley

"The kingdom of heaven and the kingdom of God on the earth will be combined together at Christ's coming - and that time is not far distant. How I wish we could get the vision of this work, the genius of it, and realize the nearness of that great event. I am sure it would have a sobering effect upon us if we realized what is before us."

Elder Ezra Taft Benson
"Should the Lord decide at this time to cleanse the Church ...a famine in this land of one year's duration could wipe out a large percentage of slothful members, including some ward and stake officers. Yet we cannot say we have not been warned." General Conference, April 1965.

Elder Dallin H. Oaks:

"We are living in the prophesied time 'when peace shall be taken from the earth' (D&C 1:35,) when 'all things shall be in commotion' and 'men's hearts shall fail them' (D&C 88:91.) There are many temporal causes of commotion, including wars and natural disasters, but an even greater cause of current 'commotion' is spiritual.

We need to make both temporal and spiritual preparation for the events prophesied at the time of the Second Coming. And the preparation most likely to be neglected is the one less visible and more difficult—the spiritual.

Elder Marion G. Romney - "...We will see the day when we will live on what we produce" General Conference April 1975.

Joseph B. Wirthlin, 1996
In terms of the sin, evil and wickedness, upon the earth, we could liken our time to the days of Noah before the flood.

Vaughn J. Featherstone, 1983 *"The darkest clouds in history are on the horizon. They are being driven with fierce Satanic winds in our direction. Earthquakes, famines pestilence, disease, plagues will soon be upon us, but we trust in our God and He will spare us and take us under His wing.*

President Boyd K. Packer, *"I am sorry to tell you that it will not get better." President Packer goes on to say: "I know of nothing in the history of the Church, or in the history of the world to compare with our present circumstances. Nothing happened in Sodom and Gomorrah which exceeds in wickedness and depravity that which surrounds us now. Words of profanity, vulgarity, and blasphemy are heard everywhere. Unspeakable wickedness and perversion were once hidden in dark places; now they are in the open, and even accorded legal protection. At Sodom and Gomorrah these things were localized. Now, they are spread across the world, and they are among us".*

"We live in turbulent times. Often the future is unknown; therefore, it behooves us to prepare for uncertainties. When the time for decision arrives, the time for preparation is past."
President Thomas S. Monson
Ensign, September 2014
"Are We Prepared?"

"There will come a time when there isn't a store."
President Spencer W. Kimball
April 1974 Gen. Conf., Welfare Session
"Family Preparedness"

"We encourage families to have on hand a year's supply; and we say it over and over and repeat over and over the scripture of the Lord where He says, 'Why call ye me, Lord, Lord, and do not the things which I say?'"
President Spencer W. Kimball
April 1974 General Conference
"Family Preparedness"

"We are living in the prophesied time "when peace shall be taken from the earth" (D&C 1:35), when "all things shall be in commotion" and "men's hearts shall fail them" (D&C 88:91)...[The] signs of the Second Coming are all around us and [are] increasing in frequency and intensity."
Elder Dallin H. Oaks
April 2004 General Conference
"Preparation for the Second Coming"

"The giant earthquake, and the tsunamis it sent crashing into the coasts around the Indian Ocean, is just the beginning and a part of what is to come..."
President Henry B. Eyring
BYU-Idaho Devotional, Jan. 25, 2005
"Raise the Bar"

Knowing there is a possibility that God will use the same pattern when the harrowing events of the end times begin, how would we prepare temporally and spiritually any different? What if you could see into the future to obtain that information?

We have been given that advantage of seeing into the future by others who have had visions, dreams or near death experiences. Church leaders, average members, and even non-members have been willing to step forward and share their experiences.

> **In Joel 2:28**
> *And it shall come to pass afterward, that I will pour out my spirit upon all flesh; and your sons and your daughters shall prophesy, your old men shall dream dreams, your young men shall see visions.*

This book was written to pull in a compilation of visions for review. It is not meant to peddle doom and gloom, but to help develop a testimony that God does protect His people and He will protect us if we do our part to prepare spiritually and temporally. Hopefully we will review our readiness, fill in the gaps and step up our game plan if need be as to be help to many others who will come to us for safety and peace.

Reading List

Books:
There is No Death, Sarah Menet
Visions of Glory, John Pontius
The Cleansing of America, Cleon Skousen
Through the Window of Life, Suzanne Freeman
A Greater Tomorrow, Julie Rowe
The Time is Now, Julie Rowe
As a Thief in the Night, Roger K. Young
65 Signs of the Time, David J. Ridges
Dreams and Visions, I & II, Roger K. Young

Recorded Visions in Church Archives:
Patriarch Charles Evans
President John Taylor
Bishop John Koyle
Heber C. Kimball
President George Albert Smith
Dream of Plagues
Cardston Prophecy

Visions from Church Members:
Alma Erickson
Moses Thatcher
Sarah Menet
Julie Rowe
Suzanne Freeman

Visions from Non LDS:
George Washington

Overview of the Primary Visions

Patriarch Charles Evans

- Fears for the State of the Union.
- Sees the tribulation period and the wickedness of the country.
- Sees multitudes fleeing to the place of safety in the mountains where the church was established.
- Confidence is lost - wealth against labor, labor against wealth.
- Sees economic collapse that triggers a civil war.
- Earthquakes begin in vast chasms all over the U.S.
- Multiple plagues are released, atmosphere is leaden hue.
- Foreign power invades the country, our men come out of the mountains to rescue the constitution and drive out the foreign troops.
- The gospel goes forth again. The New Jerusalem temple is built and becomes the center of the country.
- Details about the state of the Millennium.

President John Taylor

- Saw badges of mourning on every house in Salt Lake City (plague).
- Streets empty. People walking with bundles to get to the mountains.
- Civil war. Family against family, men killing one another, tumult.
- Washington DC, White House was empty. Everything in ruins.
- Monuments blown up.
- Water in Chesapeake Bay stagnant.
- Philadelphia everyone was dead.
- New York dead everywhere, destruction, death and rapine.
- No carriages, buggies or cars were running.
- Mighty fire raging.
- Missouri River desolate, but 12 men dressed in temple robes consecrating the ground to build the New Jerusalem temple.
- Saw people coming from the desert mountains to build the temple.
- Great pillar of clouds hovering over the temple site.

Overview of the Primary Visions Continued

Heber C. Kimball

- Army of Elders will be sent out to the four quarters to search out and warn the wicked of what is coming.
- Salt Lake City will be classed among the wicked cities of the world.
- A spirit of speculation and extravagance will take possession of the Saints, and the results will be financial bondage.
- Persecution comes next. All true LDS will be tested to the limit.
- Many will apostatize. Darkness will cover the land and the minds of the people.
- The judgments of God will be poured out on the wicked.
- Elders far and near will be called home.
- Missouri will be swept clean.
- Prophet Joseph will make an appearance to the faithful at Adam-ondi-Ahman.

President George Albert Smith

- There will be another great war that will make the Great Depression look like a Sunday picnic.
- People will drop like flies.
- Soviet Union's military will dwarf the U.S. (happened under Obama)
- U.S. withdraws its missiles from Europe (happened in 1988)
- Until then all presidents will be of British or No. European ancestry.
- Trucks will be planted along the highways and detonate all at once.
- Nuclear strikes and an EMP.
- Conditions will return to pre-1800 ancestors.
- There will be a nuclear attack on a holiday after a new president is elected (but before he takes office).

Overview of Visions Continued

Dream of Plagues

- Messenger hands him a book "Book of the Plagues".
- Feast in progress, appearance of a midsummer feast.
- Sky is a sickly brassy hue.
- Small white specs were falling from the sky into the food. So small as to be invisible to the naked eye.
- Sudden destruction had come upon them.
- Foul odor in the air. Death everywhere. Stores unlocked, dogs eating the bodies.
- "A camp of Saints who have gathered together are living under the daily revelations of God and are thus preserved from the plague."
- Saw tents in rows reaching as far as the surrounding trees, clean and white.

Cardston Prophecy

- International break out on the Pacific Ocean. (WWIII)
- Opposing forces where Christians on one side, followers of Mohammed on the other.
- Antagonism expressed towards the LDS.
- National revolution occur in every country.
- Geological disturbances.
- Boundary lines dissolve (Canadian and Mexican border).
- Race rioting on a vast scale.
- Hunger, starvation, disease, strife and chaos.
- Events continuous and ran concurrently.
- Higher spiritual beings prepare the high officials of your church, impressing them, warning them.
- Saw instructions given whereby places of refuge were prepared quietly but efficiently by the inspired elders. Vast quantities of supplies are stored up.
- A great apostasy. Hostility towards our faith.
- Vast quantities of necessaries supplied by members whose spiritual eyes had been opened. Saw a liquidation of properties and effects disposed of quietly but quickly by members of the church as the spiritual influences directed them.
- Inspired call sent forth to all the church, to gather to the refuges of Zion.

Overview of Visions Continued

Alma Erickson (1930)

- People will esteem one another according to their possession of wealth and not according to the value of the soul.
- There will be a great apostasy in the church.
- There will be poverty and starvation sweep the land.
- Money becomes increasingly worthless. US money becomes worthless.
- Gasoline will disappear and nothing shall be hauled over the rails.
- Women shall exceed the men in number.
- Flies will be sent as a plague.
- Righteous shall flee to Zion. Large crowds coming to Utah.
- Gangs will increase in numbers.
- Tornadoes shall come here in the West. High winds and cyclones.
- Ocean will become exceedingly rough, no ships can cross.
- American flag fades. Another flag (UN) appears.
- War comes on American land.
- Drops of rain as if carrying death wherever it lands.
- Northern Lights will be seen from SLC out of their regular bounds.
- Storms rage, people's bodies are now charged with a downward flow of electricity instead of upward flows. Same with food.
- Earthquakes all over the earth.
- Darkness appears during the day and it looks like the stars are falling (earth is thrown out of its regular way, sun fails to follow its true course.)
- Sees the Lost Tribes.
- Great flood in the Salt Lake Valley. Water subsides and people come back.
- Land becomes fertile again. Utah becomes a place of refuge.
- Sees Jesus Christ come in a cloud out of the East.
- Sees immortal mothers with babies in arms to raise during the Millennium.

Overview of Visions Continued

Sarah Menet

- Planes crashed into two tall buildings.
- Jars dropped (symbolic) of liquid in major cities that caused death.
- Multiple plagues.
- Looting, marauders, gangs killing people.
- Long winter following the sickness that went into the summer.
- The economy and electricity are completely gone.
- People digging for worms for food.
- Little drinking water, water was contaminated (nuclear).
- Family against family, lost family bond.
- Saw "cities of light" (tent cities) as places of refuge.
- Tent cities were established before a biological attack.
- Cities of light had food that others did not and readily shared.
- Cities were gathered in the mountains.
- Saw a missile from Libya hit Israel (Iran sent it.)
- Truck bombs go off and nuclear missiles in America.
- Fireballs from the sky started a lot of fires.
- Earthquakes in multiple places. Utah and the Mississippi River.

Suzanne Freeman

- Plagues, wet spring, joblessness and natural disasters.
- Foreign troops in America. Martial Law.
- No church meetings allowed.
- No gasoline. Trucks refused to deliver in plague zones.
- Earthquakes, volcanoes and tornadoes in America.
- Chip in hand needed to buy or sell. Must make an oath.
- Beheadings.
- Mild winter precedes a long winter.
- Several years in New Jerusalem.
- Must be selfless and willing to share to be ready to meet Christ.
- Must be able to rely 100% on the Lord.
- Lost Tribes will help Saints arrive to New Jerusalem.

Julie Rowe

- The nation was not experiencing anything major when the LDS Church scheduled a meeting concerning preparedness. An inventory was taken. Then an invitation to gather from the prophet was issued.
- The gathering places were at Church owned properties, like girl's camps.
- The majority of the church was shocked, but many had been inspired that this would happen.
- Within hours the plan was put into place. There was still electricity and cars on the road.
- The Saints moved quietly, but quickly.
- The groups left in waves within 24- 48 hours.
- Many left too late (weeks later) and could not make it there safely.
- Troop invasion limited travel.
- There were three types of camps. Tent Cities (nonmembers), Cities of Refuge (members and nonmembers), and Cities of Light (endowed members with a tent temple, ready to live the law of consecration).
- Some from the camps would later be called to go back to Missouri to build the New Jerusalem temple.
- Some gave up and left the camps only to find it very difficult when they got back to their homes.
- The camps lasted almost 2 years. Then organized again later as needed, but the camps had a shield of invisibility placed over them so the troops could not find them.
- There were pillars of smoke over the tent temples.
- The camps were well organized with gardens, security, callings, etc.
- There was death in the camps, those who lived up to their foreordained missions in life, and particularly those who suffer and are martyred for Christ's sake, will receive eternal glory we cannot now perceive.
- To view the complete chapter nine of her book, go to www.nofearpreps.com

Visions of Glory

- Earthquake off the Richter scale in Utah in the fall.
- Massive flooding with the earthquake.
- A devastating plague shows up after the earthquake.
- People were commissioned to survive.
- Airport flooded. Stopped supplies.
- People get angry with God over the quake.
- UN troops eventually get food supplies in.
- Chinese Troops show up and take over UN troops.
- Winter after the earthquake is mild.
- More earthquakes in the U.S. and around the world.
- SLC Conference flooded.
- New World Order is trying to be implemented.
- Nukes go off around the nation and Utah.
- Martial Law.
- Our spiritual preparedness helps us to see God's guiding hand.
- Water is contaminated. Starts to clear up.
- Miracles abound. Fullness of the priesthood.
- Surge in missionary work.
- No cars on the streets. (no gasoline)
- Meeting at Adam-ondi-Ahman
- Treks to Cardston Canada to attend a tent city/gathering.
- Bodies start changing to meet the trials.
- A year after the earthquake missionaries sent back out.
- Gold and Silver are worthless.
- Changes in the earth.
- Tent cities were organized before the earthquake (p.163)
- Not everyone goes to Missouri (New Jerusalem).
- No electricity. No news. No internet.
- Millennial conditions.

Common Patterns

1. Earthquake
2. Multiple Plagues
3. Economic Collapse Worldwide
4. Civil War in America
5. Foreign Troops in America/Nuclear Strikes
6. Places of Refuge protect Saints from Calamities

Summary of the Vision Books

1. Wickedness will be cleansed from the earth.
2. Our own refinement will take place so we can be prepared to meet the Savior just as saints before us.
3. Miracles will abound: food will replenish itself, people will be raised from the dead, shields of invisibility will be around tent cities to protect from the troops, water will be made clean, our men fight off troops with the wave of a hand, and more.
4. Our bodies start to change so we can endure the tribulations.
5. A new government will come about, a new society, new technologies (what we have now will seem old school), science will be settled, we will have a new mission in life as we usher in the Millennium era.
6. We will shed 100% of our possessions and rely 100% on the Savior to sustain us as the world comes to us looking for the peace, food and safety.
7. When we are not selfish, we will invoke a blessing of protection. People who do not share are cursed.
8. This is a time for celebration, not fear. Fear can actually cause harm to you.

Possibility that We will Gather Soon
5 Clues from the Visions

Timeline Possibility from the visions.

CLUE #1

President George Albert Smith's Vision:

"I have had a troublesome vision of another great and terrible war that made the war just ended look like a training exercise, and people died like flies. It began at a time when the Soviet Union's military might dwarfed that of the United States, and we, that is the United States, would have missiles that carried an atomic bomb in Europe. I saw the United States withdraw its missiles to appease the Soviet Union, and then the war began.".......<u>"Until then all the presidents would be of British or Northern European ancestry."</u>

MY COMMENTARY:

We now have a president who is not of British or Northern European ancestry. (President Smith was looking at a non-white person, not a pedigree chart, not to mention that Obama's ancestry derives from Kenya and his mother's ancestry is linked into America's first black slave in the 1600's). He also makes a statement, "He is of Greek descent." Later the nephew who recorded this statement retracted the statement. It was code for "black". During Pres. Smith's time, blacks were often called "Greeks".

OTHER CLUE:

David Horne (nephew) also mentioned that President Smith indicated that this nuclear attack would take place on a holiday <u>after the new president was elected,</u> <u>but before he took office.</u>

MY COMMENTARY:

November 2016 we will have a non-white president leaving office. *If this is not the date, we have another 4 years for another election. However, the Shemitah and Blood Moons (Tetrad) are this year. According to the Jewish Elders, this is the opening of the 7th Seal. This is the opening of the tribulation period. (See: Astronomical Odds)*

The new president will not be able to take office. This coincides with other visions that Obama will be kept at president as Martial Law is declared thus suspending the constitution. We have never had a president that has downsized our missiles over 30% , released hundreds of 4 star generals, revamped our nuclear codes, militarized local police agencies, expanded NSA spying on citizens, belittled and cut off Israel (adding to world pressure to ostracize the Jews), put a

Muslim in charge of Homeland Security, removed our immigration laws, has a shadow immigration program, used the IRS to punish political enemies, constructed 23 FEMA camps (still empty, but fully stocked), seized control of our healthcare on a federal level, restricts guns and ammo by executive order, talks of redistribution of wealth and collective salvation, ignores the terrorism foisted on our military/political interests (embassies), armed drug cartels on the border, made executive orders to allow for abortion into the 3rd trimester, wrote in his book if the winds of change go against the Muslims, his sympathies will lie with them, attended a black liberation theology church for 20 years, criticizes Britain and the US for "colonizing" other countries, was raised by a registered communist party mother and step-father and ultimately ran up an addition 10 trillion dollars of debt (we can't even pay back the first 2) while in office. (See section "Jon McNaughton's, Obama's Foreign Policy").

CLUE #2

Troops show up at the end of the Utah earthquake. (Earthquake is in October 2016)

Spencer (Visions of Glory):

There had been a massive earthquake in that area in the <u>fall</u> of the year.

.....We took materials from damaged homes to repair the standing ones. Many families moved in together into one home. It was a herculean effort. ....

<u>About this time a large column of military vehicles arrived in town</u>. They had come to help. They wore blue helmets, and had UN symbols on their doors and insignia on their helmets and uniforms. Our local civic leaders had tried to organize relief efforts, but that effort collapsed <u>when the foreign troops took over</u>.

The foreign troops were from many nations. Most groups didn't speak English at all. There were groups who looked Asian or Chinese. We couldn't tell from their language or from their uniforms because they were all dressed alike.

I never saw a full column of U.S soldiers or National Guard. I found out later that atomic weapons had been deployed to take out major defense installations around the nation and in Utah. They had been a first strike against the United States, and came without provocation.

<u>About this time the same plague which had devastated so much of the east coast arrived in Utah as it spread across the nation.</u> The foreign troops had brought hazmat equipment, as if they were expecting the plague, and very few of them got sick. As I said, we found out later that the plague was man-made, and the troops had been inoculated against the pathogen that caused the plague.

MY COMMENTARY

Spencer says the troops arrive while they are cleaning up from the earthquake. We know from other visions that the earthquake is in the fall/October of xxxx year. If the troops show up after a November election, then the earthquake is in October of 2016.

CLUE #3

Economic Collapse - SEPTEMBER 2016 - Which triggers Civil War
Notice the economic collapse is right before the earthquake.
A dollar collapse is not the same as a stock market collapse. (Stock market collapse is in 2015 as per Shemitah Year - See: Astronomical Odds.)

Spencer (VoG):

I saw that whenever this time was that I was being shown, that the financial structure of the world had completely collapsed. Every bank had closed down and money was worthless. People were learning to trade and barter. Manufacturing and industry were at a virtual standstill. There were no raw materials, and no money to pay the workers. Factories and global businesses shut down overnight.

All of the utilities were in chaos. People tried to keep the necessities of life running, but they were sporadic and mostly off-line. There were blackouts everywhere, some of them lasting many months. Almost all water was not fit to drink because of acts of war against this country. People suffered everywhere.

My flight across North America began in Salt Lake City. There had been a massive earthquake in that area in the fall of the year.

Charles Evans (Church Archives) 1894

Confidence is lost. Wealth is arrayed against labor, labor against wealth....together with the policy of many wealthy ones, has produced distress and do presage further sorrow. Mad with rage men and women rushed upon each other. Blood flowed down the streets of cities like water.

Sols Caurdisto The Cardston Prophecy 1923 (Church Archives)

I saw the international world war automatically break down, and national revolution occur in every country and complete the work of chaos and desolation. ...I saw the international boundary line disappear (Cananda/US) and these two governments broke up and dissolved into chaos. I saw race rioting upon the American continent on a vast scale.

Sarah Menet, There is no Death

Shopping and buying seemed to stop and the economy failed throughout the world. Few had any money at all, and those who did have it could not buy anything. Gold and silver and other commodities had value and could be traded.

Gayle Smith (personal dream/story on internet) 1993 (Gayle has since been excommunicated, but at the time of her vision she was in full standing.)

My mother then started showing me a scenario of events that will take place beginning with a worldwide economic collapse that would take place in the month of October.

I was told it will actually begin in the US. The reason it happens is to bring down America. I don't think they want to destroy America, they just want to bring it under their control. My mother said I would hear rumors and they will get louder and the collapse will happen quickly. We will wake up one morning and it will have happened.

After the collapse I saw marauding bands or gangs running around. People just go crazy and start rioting. They are killing because they are angry and hungry. Everything they know of value on this earth is being taken away from them within a few days. In a very short time there will be a famine.
..... A short period of time after the economic collapse we are put under the control of FEMA and martial law. The first thing they do is to close down all the roads and accesses out of the cities. Next they cut communications and conduct house to house searches for food, guns and ammunition. I saw them taking warm boots and warm clothing because it was getting cold and winter was coming. The martial law is so oppressive..... The next scenario I was shown was during the first earthquake in a building with some friends. I knew the building wasn't safe with the earthquake. I opened the door, looked outside and saw the trees falling like dominos all over.

CLUE #4

Plague is released (probably in July 2016).
SAINTS IN CAMPS JUST BEFORE THAT RELEASE (SPRING 2016)

Dream of Plagues: (Church Archives)

Below this scene was the description: <u>A Feast</u> among the Gentiles, commencement of the Plague. And in smaller type below a note saying that the particles of poison, though represented in the picture, are so small as to be invisible to the naked eye.

Again it was a <u>midsummer</u> scene. The same atoms of poison were falling through the air, but their work was done; the same sickly brazen atmosphere that seemed thick with foul odors laid upon the earth, in which no breeze stirred a leaf of the foliage. Upon the balconies of the richly decorated residences, across the thresholds of the open doorways, along the walks and upon the crossings, lay the men, women and children, who a few days before were enjoying all the pleasures of life. Further on, the dead were everywhere. ....

Below this picture was the description: "<u>A camp of the Saints who have gathered together and are living under the daily revelations of God, and are thus preserved from the plague.</u>" I understood from this that each family was in its tent during the hours of the day that the poison falls, and thus were preserved from breathing the deathly particles.

Sols Caurdisto – The Cardston Prophecy (Church Archives)

I saw the other officials obeying the inspired instructions, carrying their message and exhorting the people to carry out, from time to time the revelation given them, whilst all around throughout the Gentile world the chaos developed in its varying stages, faction against faction, nation against nation, but all in open or secret hostility to your people and their faith. I saw your people draw closer and closer together, as this became more tense and as the spiritual forces warned them through the mouth of your elders and your other officers. I saw the spiritual forces influencing those members who had drifted away, to re-enter the fold. I saw a greater tithing than ever before. I saw vast quantities of necessaries supplied by members whose spiritual eyes had been opened. I saw a liquidation of properties and effects disposed of quietly but quickly by members of the church, as the spiritual influences directed them.

I saw the inspired call sent forth to all the church, to gather to the refuges of Zion. I saw the stream of your people quietly moving in the direction of their refuge. I saw your people moving more quickly and in larger numbers until all the stragglers were housed. I saw the wireless message flashed from Zion's refuge to Zion's refuge in their several places that all was well with them, and then the darkness of chaos closed around the boundaries of your people, and the last days of tribulation had begun.

Charles Evans (Church Archives)

My vision now became extended in a marvelous manner, and the import of the past labors of the Elders was made plain to me. I saw multitudes fleeing to the place of safety in our mountain heights. The church was established in the wilderness. ...
"But," continued the messenger, Thou beholdest a change. Confidence is lost. Wealth is arrayed against labor, labor against wealth, yet the land abounds with plenty for food and raiment, and silver and gold are in abundance. Thou seest also that letters written by a Jew have wrought great confusion in the finances of the nation which, together with the policy of many wealthy ones, has produced distress and do presage further sorrow."

Factions now sprang up as if by magic; capital had entrenched itself against labor throughout the land; labor was organized against capital. The voice of the wise sought to tranquilize these two powerful factors in vain. Excited multitudes ran wildly about; strikes increased; lawlessness sought the place of regular government. At this juncture I saw a banner floating in air whereon was written the words Bankruptcy, Famine, Floods, Fire, Cyclones, Blood, Plague. Mad with rage men and women rushed upon each other. Blood flowed down the streets of cities like water. The demon of bloody hate had enthroned itself on the citadel of reason; the thirst for blood was intenser than that of the parched tongue for water. Thousands of bodies lay untombed in the streets
...Earthquakes rent the earth in vast chasms, which engulfed multitudes; terrible groanings and wailings filled the air; the shrieks of the suffering were indescribably awful.
...missiles were hurled through the atmosphere at a terrible velocity and people were carried upward only to descend in unrecognized mass
... men fell exhausted, appalled and trembling. Every element of agitated nature seemed a demon of wrathful fury.

...Again the light shone, revealing an atmosphere tinged with a leaden hue, which was the precursor of an unparalleled plague whose first symptoms were recognized by a purple spot which appeared on the cheek, or on the back of the hand, and which, invariably, enlarged until it spread over the entire surface of the body, producing certain death

Clue #5
The Church possibly issues a call to gather in Spring of 2016

Sarah Menet

As I looked upon this scene of chaos, smoke, and destruction, I noticed there were small pockets of light scattered over the US, perhaps 20 or 30 of them. I noticed that most of the locations of light were in the western part of the US with only three of four of them being in the East. These places of light seemed to shine brightly through the darkness and were such a contrast to the rest of the scene that they caught my full attention. I focused on them for a moment and asked, "What is this light?"

I was then able to see these points of light were people who had gathered together and were kneeling in prayer. The light was actually coming from the people, and I understood that it was showing forth their goodness and love for each other. They had gathered together for safety and contrary to what I had witnessed elsewhere were caring more for each other than for themselves. Some of the groups were small with only a hundred people or so. Other groups consisted of what seemed to be thousands.

I realized that many, if not all, of these places of light, or "cities of light" had somehow been established just before the biological attack and they were very organized. In these places were relative peace and safety. I noticed the gangs made no threats on these groups. However, the people within had defenses and God was with them.

The Cardston Prophecy (1923)

I saw further on, instructions given whereby places of refuge prepared quietly but efficiently by inspired elders. I saw Cardston and the surrounding foothills, especially north and west for miles, being prepared for your people quietly but quickly. I saw the fuel resources of the district develop in many places and vast piles of coal and timber stored for future use and building. I saw the territory carefully surveyed and mapped out, for the camping of a great body of the people of the church. I saw provision also made for a big influx of people who will not at first belong to the church , but who will gather in their tribulation. I saw these things going on practically unknown to the Gentile world.

I saw the inspired call sent forth to all the church, to gather to the refuges of Zion. I saw the stream of your people quietly moving in the direction of their refuge. I saw your people moving more quickly in larger numbers until all the stragglers were housed. I saw the wireless message flashed from Zion's refuge to Zion's refuge in their several places that all was well with them, and then the darkness of chaos closed around the boundaries of your people, and the last days of tribulation had begun.

Anonymous (Dream & Visions Volume II, p.124)

I would note that during this part of the dream, when we initially left, there was no sense of panic or urgency. We were hurrying to get going because we didn't want to be left behind. Also, I was told that some people were asked to go, but didn't want to. From this I infer that the conditions of the or the US, were so based as to make it an easy decision as whether to stay or leave.

Anyway, after a while, we all gathered together in a central area and were welcomed by President Monson and not President Hinckley there, remember this dream occurred in approximately the year 2000.

Frequently Asked Questions about a "Call Out"

1. **What is a call out?** The term is interchangeable with "gathering", "tent cities", "places of refuge" or any other reference to the saints coming together, at the prophet's invitation to avoid an upcoming devastation or calamity.

2. **Are there references from the general authorities concerning these gatherings?** Yes, here are just a few:

    Henry B. Eyring - Raise the Bar (BYU-Idaho Talk - January 2005) *Fear shall come upon all people. But you and I know that the Lord has prepared <u>places of safety</u> to which he is eager to guide us....It will be our choice whether or not to move up or stay where we are. But the Lord will invite and guide us upward by the direction of the Holy Ghost....*

    Harold B. Lee Conference Report, April 1948

    Thus, clearly, the Lord has placed the responsibility for directing the work of gathering in the hands of the leaders of the Church to whom he will reveal his will where and <u>when such gatherings would take place in the future.</u>

    It would be well before the frightening events concerning the fulfillment of all God's promises and predictions are upon us, that the Saints in every land prepare themselves and look forward to the instruction that shall <u>come to them from the First Presidency of this Church</u> as to where they shall be gathered and not be disturbed in their feelings until such instruction is given to them as it is revealed by the Lord to the proper authority.

3. ***Is there biblical support for such an activity?*** *Yes, it is a pattern that the Lord calls out his people just before destroying or cleansing the wicked.*

    > *Enoch - Increased wars and bloodshed, secret combinations*
    > *Noah - Destruction of all of the wicked*
    > *Abraham - First time...Wickedness in Ur, fled to save life*
    > *Lot - Destruction of Sodom & Gomorrah by fire from heaven*
    > *Israel/Joseph - Terrible famines (moved to Egypt)*
    > *Moses - Slavery under Egyptians*
    > *Lehi - Destruction of Jerusalem because of wickedness*
    > *Nephi - Destruction at hand of wicked brothers*

4. **Are there scriptures that identify a gathering for refuge in the last days?** Yes, here are just a few:

*Yea, they shall not be beaten down by the storm at the last day; yea, neither shall they be harrowed up by the whirlwinds; but when the storm cometh <u>they shall be gathered together in their place</u>, that the storm cannot penetrate to them; yea, neither shall they be driven with fierce winds whithersoever the enemy listeth to carry them. But behold, they are in the hands of the Lord of the harvest, and they are his; and he will raise them up at the last day. Blessed be the name of the our God; let us sing to his praise, yea, let us give thanks to his holy name, for he doth work righteousness forever. **Alma 26: 5-8***

*For the Lord shall comfort Zion, he will comfort all her waste places; and he will make her wilderness like Eden, and her desert like the garden of the Lord. Joy and gladness shall be found therein, thanksgiving and the voice of melody. **Isaiah 51:3***

*For in this mountain shall the hand of the Lord rest, and Moab shall be trodden down under him, even as straw is trodden down for the dunghill. **Isaiah 25:10***

*But thus saith the Lord: Even the captives of the mighty shall be taken away, and the prey of the terrible shall be delivered; for the Mighty God shall deliver his covenant people. For thus saith the Lord: I will contend with them that contendeth with thee--**2 Nephi 6:17***

Wherefore the decree hath gone forth from the Father that <u>they shall be gathered in unto one place upon the face of this land</u>, to prepare their hearts and be prepared in all things against the day when tribulation and desolation are sent forth upon the wicked.

*For the hour is nigh and the day soon at hand when the earth is ripe; and all the proud and they that do wickedly shall be as stubble; and I will burn them up, saith the Lord of Hosts, that wickedness shall not be upon the earth; **D&C 8:8-9***

5. **Why don't we talk about this in church?** There many things that cannot be discussed and we must protect ourselves. However, we can know if these things are true simply by asking for our own personal confirmation.

D&C 45:72 And now I say unto you, keep these things from going abroad unto the world until it is expedient in me, that ye may accomplish this work in the eyes of the people, and in the eyes of your enemies, that they may not know your works until ye have accomplished the thing which I have commanded you;

Matthew Chapter 24
Christ Tells Us What Signs to Watch For
My comments are in green.

1 And Jesus went out, and departed from the temple: and his disciples came to him for to shew him the buildings of the temple.

2 And Jesus said unto them, See ye not all these things? verily I say unto you, There shall not be left here one stone upon another, that shall not be thrown down.

3 ¶And as he sat upon the mount of Olives, the disciples came unto him privately, saying, Tell us, when shall these things be? and <u>what shall be the sign of thy coming</u>, and of the end of the world?

4 And Jesus answered and said unto them, Take heed that no man deceive you. *Beware of false Christs.*

5 For many shall come in my name, saying, I am Christ; and shall deceive many.

6 And ye shall hear of wars and rumours of wars: see that ye be not troubled: for all these things must come to pass, but the end is not yet. <u>There will be wars, do not be troubled.</u>

As of Sept 2014, the U.S. is involved in 134 conflicts or "wars" around the world.

The US Is Now Involved In 134 Wars

Or none, depending on your definition of 'war'.

By Timothy McGrath | September 22, 2014

http://www.mintpressnews.com/us-now-involved-134-wars/196846/

7 For nation shall rise against nation, and kingdom against kingdom: and there shall be <u>famines, and pestilences, and earthquakes</u>, in divers places.

Wheat Shortage in America and the World

By Kellene Bishop, Preparedness Pro on 3 June 2009 - 1:00pm

By Kellene Bishop

While I reported on the looming wheat shortage in detail several months ago, it has caught my attention again due to how quickly

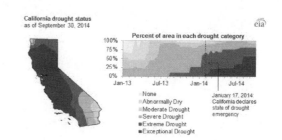

http://www.preparednesspro.com/wheat-shortage-in-america-and-the-world
http://www.eia.gov/todayinenergy/detail.cfm?id=18271 (CA feeds 25% of the world, 70% of the U.S., 55,000 farms have shut down, cattle moved to TX, no water for hay.)

Earthquakes are increasing:

Current disease/plague outbreaks in 2015.

http://earthquake.usgs.gov/earthquakes/?source=sitenav
http://outbreaks.globalincidentmap.com/

8 All these are the <u>beginning</u> of sorrows.

9 Then shall they deliver you up to be afflicted, and shall kill you: and ye shall be hated of all nations for my name's sake.

Notice the parallel between what is prophesied for Israel is also prophesied for the LDS.
Israel needs to build a temple, we will build the New Jerusalem temple.
Israel will be under siege (Armageddon), we will be under siege (foreign troops).
Israel is told to flee to the mountains, we are told to flee to the mountains.
Israel is persecuted and hated, we will be persecuted and hated. (Much more to come.)

10 And then shall many be offended, and shall betray one another, and shall hate one another.
Race wars, political divisions, and religious divisions are under way.

http://www.washingtonpost.com/wp-srv/style/longterm/books/chap1/comingracewar.htm

11 And many false prophets shall rise, and shall deceive many.

12 And because iniquity shall abound, the love of many shall wax cold.

Domestic violence is the leading cause of injury to women between the ages of 15 and 44 in the United States, more than car accidents, muggings, and rapes combined. ("Violence Against Women, A Majority Staff Report," Committee on the Judiciary, United States Senate, 102nd Congress, October 1992, p.3.)

13 But he that shall endure unto the end, the same shall be saved.

14 And this gospel of the kingdom shall be preached in all the world for a witness unto all nations; and then shall the end come.

Gospel preached to all the nations (considered fulfilled by the advent of the internet), 80,000 missionaries a year, it took 100 years to get 98 stakes, we currently have over 3,000 stakes. We are currently in the "hastening" (President Monson).

15 When ye therefore shall see the abomination of desolation, spoken of by Daniel the prophet, stand in the holy place, (whoso readeth, let him understand:)

16 Then let them which be in Judæa flee into the mountains:

Flee to the mountains, stand in holy places (1st call out, you will be able to get there with vehicles and relative safety). You will need to be following the prophet to hear about it and be active enough (possibly temple going) to embrace such a directive from the prophet

17 Let him which is on the housetop not come down to take any thing out of his house:

Don't go back for your things.

18 Neither let him which is in the field return back to take his clothes.

19 And woe unto them that are with child, and to them that give suck in those days!

It will be bad for pregnant women and babies.

20 But pray ye that your flight be not in the winter, neither on the sabbath day:

Don't wait until winter to flee - people who missed the 1st call out will have to walk and not be able to take many preparations with them and there will not have much safety.

21 For then shall be great tribulation, such as was not since the beginning of the world to this time, no, nor ever shall be.

Greatest tribulation ever will begin - See Cardston Prophecy (last line)....as soon as all the stragglers are in (tent cities) the darkness of chaos closed around them and the last days of tribulation begins.

22 And except those days should be shortened, there should no flesh be saved: but for the elect's sake those days shall be shortened.

No one survives unless the days are shortened (7 year tribulation).

23 Then if any man shall say unto you, Lo, here is Christ, or there; believe it not.

Don't listen to people who say Christ is here. (remember he comes from the clouds for all to see.) Here is a current example of a false christ.

Maitreya as he appeared in Nairobi, in 1988

This is the man the UN has sponsored to be the next world president. Maitreya performs miracles, says he is Jesus Christ, the 12 Imam (Muslims) and the Messiah (Jews) the world has been waiting for all rolled into one. He appears and disappears out of thin air. Go to link below for UN Share Magazine and read all the glowing comments how this person will save the world soon.

Then watch this video of a girl who sees the anti-Christ in a vision and everyone worships this guy named "Maitreya".
https://www.youtube.com/watch?v=1LFNmNLBOFE

http://www.share-international.org/maitreya/Ma_main.htm

24 For there shall arise false Christs, and false prophets, and shall shew great signs and wonders; insomuch that, if <u>it were possible</u>, they shall deceive the very elect. (Elect = endowed. Notice "if")

25 Behold, I have told you before.

26 Wherefore if they shall say unto you, Behold, he is in the desert; go not forth: behold, he is in the secret chambers; believe it not.

27 For as the lightning cometh out of the east, and shineth even unto the west; so shall also the coming of the Son of man be.

Christ comes from the east in the clouds.

28 For wheresoever the carcase is, there will the eagles be gathered together.

29 ¶Immediately <u>after the tribulation</u> of those days shall the sun be darkened, and the moon shall not give her light, and the stars shall fall from heaven, and the powers of the heavens shall be shaken:

A good sign that the tribulation is coming to an end. The sun darkened is not only an eclipse, but when the earth is out of its bounds, the day will appear dark, the moon will be gone, thus the stars appearing to fall. This might explain it:

https://www.youtube.com/watch?v=0jHsq36_NTU
http://www.foxnews.com/science/2014/10/21/earth-magnetic-field-could-flip-in-our-lifetime/

30 And then shall appear the sign of the Son of man in heaven: and then shall all the tribes of the earth mourn, and they shall see the Son of man coming in the clouds of heaven with power and great glory.

31 And he shall send his angels with a great sound of a trumpet, <u>and they shall gather together his elect from the four winds</u>, from one end of heaven to the other.

Note, it says, one end of HEAVEN to the other. This is the resurrection and rising up to meet the Lord.

32 Now learn a parable of the fig tree; <u>When his branch is yet tender, and putteth forth leaves, ye know that summer is nigh</u>:

Bible scholars agree, this is symbolic for Israel. When she has gathered again and being productive, his return is soon. He says within one generation. The Jews took possession of Israel in 1948, however they didn't take possession of Jerusalem until 1967 in the 6-day war.

33 So likewise ye, when ye shall see all these things, know that it is near, even at the doors.

34 Verily I say unto you, This generation shall not pass, till all these things be fulfilled.

Since the Jews took possession of Jerusalem in 1967 it will be one generation (Bible dictionary says 1 generation = up to 70 years)...not much longer, we have up to 2037 for Christ's words to fulfill about his return.

35 Heaven and earth shall pass away, but my words shall not pass away.

36 ¶But of that day and hour knoweth no man, no, not the angels of heaven, but my Father only.

No man knoweth the day nor hour, time line is fluid to consider agency. Not even the angels know. However, we have been told we can watch for the "season" and the "signs".

37 But as the days of Noe were, so shall also the coming of the Son of man be.

38 For as in the days that were before the flood they were eating and drinking, marrying and giving in marriage, until the day that Noe entered into the ark,

39 And knew not until the flood came, and took them all away; so shall also the coming of the Son of man be.

Just like Noah's time, people not watching, don't care, or think it is further away. Christ describes himself as "thief in the night". You wake up and everything is gone.

40 Then shall two be in the field; the one shall be taken, and the other left.

41 Two women shall be grinding at the mill; the one shall be taken, and the other left.

"Rapture" - actually the "Call Out" (people will up and leave/disappear from society)

42 ¶Watch therefore: for ye know not what hour your Lord doth come.

43 But know this, that if the goodman of the house had known in what watch the thief would come, he would have watched, and would not have suffered his house to be broken up.

If you were watching, you will not be caught unaware and will have prepared.

44 Therefore be ye also ready: for in such an hour as ye think not the Son of man cometh.

45 Who then is a faithful and wise servant, whom his lord hath made ruler over his household, to give them meat in due season?

The Lord will bless you for "prepping" if you are faithful and wise. He will give you meat in due season.

46 Blessed is that servant, whom his lord when he cometh shall find so doing.

47 Verily I say unto you, <u>That he shall make him ruler over all his goods.</u>

Physical and spiritual preppers are made rulers over their goods and given protection. Don't let rumors of turning your food in or living the united order bother you. You will be made ruler over your goods. You will want to "share" as you are being "refined and tested" on your journey to meet the Savior.

48 But and if that evil servant shall say in his heart, My lord delayeth his coming;

49 And shall begin to smite his fellowservants, and to eat and drink with the drunken;

50 The lord of that servant shall come in a day when he looketh not for him, and in an hour that he is not aware of,

51 And shall cut him asunder, and appoint him his portion with the hypocrites: there shall be weeping and gnashing of teeth.

If you doubt him, the Lord will discount you and give your portion to others. He will not bless you and leave you to the hypocrites.

The Lords Signs Are Here

ASTRONOMICAL ODDS

But, behold, I say unto you that <u>before this great day shall come</u> the sun shall be darkened, and the moon shall be turned into blood, and the stars shall fall from heaven, and there shall be greater signs in heaven above and in the earth beneath; (Doctrine and Covenants 29:14)

Regular Jewish Holy Days in 2015

<u>Feast of Trumpets</u> - (Rosh Hashanah) Jewish "new year" on the calendar. No work is to be performed. Solemn preparation for the Day of Atonement.

<u>Day of Atonement</u> - (Yom Kippur) Day of fasting and repentance. *'On this day, the day of Atonement, those whom God finds worthy, are inscribed in the Book of Life.'* Those not worthy are turned over to judgment.

<u>Feast of Tabernacles</u> - (Sukkot) The most joyous of the ancient Holy Days, when having the presence of the Lord and His Tabernacle with us brings peace, rest, and great blessings. Symbolically it means joyous day, return of the King.

Here are Jewish Holy Days that are not annual, but will show up in 2015!!

<u>Shemitah Year</u> - Every SEVEN years is a rest year in which the fields lie fallow. The crops are not sown or harvested and the trees and vineyards are not pruned. Shemitah in Hebrew means "collapse". The **number 7** means completion and termination, and is of great significance.

<u>Jubilee Year</u> - SEVEN Shemitah's are a Jubilee (**or 49 years).**

<u>70th Jubilee</u> - **SEVEN Jubilees equals a Jubilee Cycle.** The 70th Jubilee, on the Jewish calendar is a much anticipated and celebrated year. (See story of Jericho.) Opening of the 7th Seal. Start of the tribulation period.

Now look what else shows up in 2015!!

<u>A Tetrad</u> is when four blood moons (moon looks red) show up together. There have only been seven tetrads since Christ. We are currently in the middle of a tetrad and *we will not see another tetrad for 500 years*. This current tetrad falls on four Jewish Holy Days!!!

Look what happened on the last seven tetrads (major Jewish historical periods):

162 - 163 Persecution of Jews and Christians... by Rome

795 - 796 Rome and Islam battle for dominance

842 - 843 Vatican attacked by African Islamic invasion

860 - 861 Islam unable to advance into Europe

1493 - 1494 Jews expelled from Spain

1949 - 1950 Rebirth of Israel, freedom from the Arabs

1967 - 1968 6 day war, victory over their Arab enemies

<u>Solar Eclipse</u> - Two of the Holy Days in 2015 will have solar eclipses.

Now look at what has happened the last two Shemitah years in our country:
2001 (9-11/markets collapsed),
2008 (housing and market collapse.
Both happened in September, and the last seven stock market collapses were exactly seven years apart and in the month of September, including the Great Depression collapse. .

The Shemitah, Jubilee and 70th Jubilee all come in September of 2015!!

These Holy Days mark the start of the tribulation. The number seven implies **completeness, perfection, to complete, to end, to fulfill.** The word translated as **'finished'** is the Greek teléo, which generally means to bring to a **close**.

http://2fletchdr222.blogspot.com/2014/04/the-history-of-8-blood-moon-tetrads.html

"Obama Foreign Policy,"

by Jon McNaughton

Is the world a safer place since Obama was made President of the United States?
I felt a need to paint a new image to capture the delicate situation we face as Americans.

What has happened since he's been in office?

Where is the stability and peace in Egypt, Libya, Syria, Yemen, Iraq, Afghanistan, Pakistan, Crimea, Ukraine, Russia, Iran, Israel, Palestine, China and North Korea? How are our veterans doing?

Are American citizens safer as they travel abroad?

When the balance of the world seems to stand on the edge of a knife, where is our President?
I hope this painting will not become prophetic in its meaning.

Since Obama has been President he has played over 200 rounds of golf.

THIS is not a game.
This is Obama's Foreign Policy."

What has he done?
· Weakened Egypt and the rise of the Arab spring. http://solutions.heritage.org/middle-east/
http://foreignpolicy.com/.../why-obama-failed-in-the-middle-.../

· Toppled Libya, which led to the emboldening of Al Qaida and the Benghazi Massacre.
http://www.washingtonpost.com/.../marc-thiessen-where-was-oba...-

http://www.breitbart.com/.../the-6-biggest-lies-about-bengha.../ diarist/2014/05/12/70c6b898-d9cc-11e3-bda1-9b46b2066796_story.html

· Embarrassment in Syria and the "red line." http://www.cnn.com/2013/09/09/opinion/cupp-obama-syria/

· Gave away multiple Guantanamo Bay prisoners who returned to ISIS and Al Qaida for an AWOL soldier who caused the lives of American servicemen.
http://www.judicialwatch.org/.../reports-show-danger-releasi.../

· Demoralized our military and has done little or nothing to strengthen the VA hospitals even after exposed corruption. http://militaryadvantage.military.com/.../why-is-the-va-scan.../

· Removed missiles from Ukraine and opened the door to Russian forces. http://www.politifact.com/.../romney-obama-stopped-missile-d.../

· Emboldened Iran's nuclear plans at Israel's expense. http://www.washingtonpost.com/.../4b80fd92-abda-11e4-ad71-7b9...

· Continued to insult Israel and create a volatile environment in the Middle East. http://www.politico.com/.../barack-obama-benjamin-netanyahu-i...

· Done little to oppose North Korea. http://www.cnn.com/.../robert-menendez-hits-obama-on-north-k.../

· Removed troops from Iraq without an exit strategy. http://www.foreignaffairs.com/.../rick-br.../withdrawal-symptoms

· Removal of troops from Afghanistan without an exit strategy. http://www.washingtonpost.com/.../fd935084-facd-11e3-b1f4-8e7...

· Improper use of drones in Pakistan and Yemen with many civilian casualties. http://www.washingtonsblog.com/.../american-drones-killed-civ...

· Killing of American citizens abroad in the name of national security. http://www.nytimes.com/.../04/07/world/middleeast/07yemen.html

· Soft on ISIS in the wake of horrific attacks in the Middle East. http://www.nairaland.com/1890136/why-obama-soft-isis

· Insistence not to mention radical Islam as a major threat to American interests. http://conservativetribune.com/oliver-north-enemy-radical-.../

Israel and the End Times

There will be a mass return of Jews to the land of Israel (Deuteronomy 30:3; Isaiah 43:6; Ezekiel 34:11-13; 36:24; 37:1-14).
This is considered fulfilled in 1948 after the Holocaust. Again in 1967 when Israel took control of Jerusalem after the 6 day war was launched on them by the Arabs.

The Antichrist will make a 7-year covenant of "peace" with Israel (Isaiah 28:18; Daniel 9:27).
The Antichrist will break his covenant with Israel, and worldwide persecution of Israel will result (Daniel 9:27; 12:1, 11; Zechariah 11:16; Matthew 24:15, 21; Revelation 12:13). Israel will be invaded (Ezekiel chapters 38-39).
See Maitreya who is being sponsored by the UN right now.
http://www.youtube.com/watch?v=KHZXlz7Rxyc

The temple will be rebuilt in Jerusalem (Daniel 9:27; Matthew 24:15; 2 Thessalonians 2:3-4; Revelation 11:1).
Jewish Elders have now drawn up the plans and are collecting artifacts to conduct temple rites. The Dome of the Rock is in the way, but the Jews are counting on God to make a way for them to build it when the time comes.
http://www.templeinstitute.org/

Israel will finally recognize Jesus as their Messiah (Zechariah 12:10). Israel will be regenerated, restored, and regathered (Jeremiah 33:8; Ezekiel 11:17; Romans 11:26).

Numbers 24:9 ....." Blessed is he that blesseth thee, and cursed is he that curseth thee."

Isaiah 54:17
No weapon that is formed against thee shall prosper; and every tongue that shall rise against thee in judgment thou shalt condemn. This is the heritage of the servants of the Lord, and their righteousness is of me, saith the Lord.

Zechariah 14:2-3, 12
2 For I will gather all nations against Jerusalem to battle; and the city shall be taken, ...and half of the city shall go forth into captivity, and the residue of the people shall not be cut off from the city.

3 Then shall the Lord go forth, and fight against those nations, as when he fought in the day of battle.

12 And this shall be the plague wherewith the Lord will smite **all the people that have fought against Jerusalem**; their flesh shall consume away while they stand upon their feet, and their eyes shall consume away in their holes, and
their tongue shall consume away in their mouth.

History of the Israeli/Palestinian Conflict

1. Israel became a nation in 1312 BCE, two thousand years before the rise of Islam.

2. Arab refugees in Israel began identifying themselves as part of a Palestinian people in 1967, *two decades after the establishment of the modern State of Israel.*

3. Since the Jewish conquest in 1272 BCE, the Jews have had dominion over the land for one thousand years with a continuous presence in the land for the past 3,300 years.

4. The only Arab dominion since the conquest in 635 CE lasted no more than 22 years.

5. For over 3,300 years, Jerusalem has been the Jewish capital Jerusalem has never been the capital of any Arab or Muslim entity. Even when the Jordanians occupied Jerusalem, they never sought to make it their capital, and Arab leaders did not come to visit.

6. Jerusalem is mentioned over 700 times in Tanach, the Jewish Holy Scriptures. Jerusalem is not mentioned once in the Koran.

7. King David founded the city of Jerusalem. Mohammed never came to Jerusalem.

8. Jews pray facing Jerusalem. Muslims pray with their backs toward Jerusalem.

9. In 1948 the Arab refugees were encouraged to leave Israel by Arab leaders promising to purge the land of Jews. Sixty-eight percent left without ever seeing an Israeli soldier.

10. The Jewish refugees were forced to flee from Arab lands due to Arab brutality, persecution, and slaughter.

11. The number of Arab refugees who left Israel in 1948 is estimated to be around 630,000. The number of Jewish refugees from Arab lands is estimated to be the same.

12. Arab refugees were **intentionally** not absorbed or integrated into the Arab lands to which they fled, despite the vast Arab territory. *Out of the 100,000,000 refugees since World War II, theirs is the only refugee group in the world that has never been absorbed or integrated into their own people's lands.* Jewish refugees were completely absorbed into Israel, a country **no larger than** the state of **New Jersey.**

13. The Arabs are represented by eight separate nations, not including the Palestinians. There is only one Jewish nation. **The Arab nations initiated all five wars and lost.** Israel defended itself each time and won.

14. **The PLO's Charter still calls for the destruction of the State of Israel.** Israel has given the Palestinians most of the West Bank land, autonomy under the Palestinian Authority, and has supplied them with police and weapons.

15. Under Jordanian rule, Jewish holy sites were desecrated and the Jews were denied access to places of worship. Under Israeli rule, all Muslim and Christian sites have been preserved and made accessible to people of all faiths.

16. The UN Record on Israel and the Arabs: of the 175 Security Council resolutions passed before 1990, 97 were directed against Israel.

17. Of the 690 General Assembly resolutions voted on before 1990, 429 were directed against Israel.

18. *The UN was silent while 58 Jerusalem Synagogues were destroyed by the Jordanians.*

19. The UN was silent while the Jordanians systematically desecrated the ancient Jewish cemetery on the Mount of Olives.

20. The UN was silent while the Jordanians enforced an apartheid-like a policy of preventing Jews from visiting the Temple Mount and the Western Wall.

21. The Israelis purchased the empty lands from the Turks, starting in 1850s. The Turks were glad to get rid of it because it was worthless. Within 20 years, the Israelis, through some monumentally hard work, got parts of it back into agricultural production.

22. Workers migrated from other areas of the Ottoman Empire to work for the Israelis. (These were renamed Palestinians in 1962 by Arafat). They didn't "own the land" nor have a presence there prior to the Israelis terraforming. Until 1962, they were called by their ethnicity: Egyptians, Syrians, Hashemites, etc.

23. The San Remo 1920 treaty graciously "gave" the Israelis the lands they had already purchased and included all of what is now Jordan. The **UK reneged on the treaty** provisions and "gave" most of the land to the Hashemites and the Palestinians, and that area is now called Jordan.

24. The Muslim workers were asked to stay and help when the Arab nations invaded in 1948. Many did and are Arab Israelis with full citizenship and rights that other Arabs can only dream of. The others didn't and became what were later known as Palestinians.

25. Israel was attacked by its Arab neighbors in coordinated wars in 1948, 1956, 1967, and 1973. In each case, those attacks were defeated.

26. Arab and Jewish refugees: Arabs were not driven out of their homes. Following the UN decision on Partition in 1948, the Arab refugees were encouraged to leave Israel by Arab leaders, promising to purge the land of Jews.
They argued that an "Arab presence" would only get in the way of the planned devastation. Sixty-eight percent left without ever seeing an Israeli soldier.

27. The "Palestinians" (or Hamas, the political arm), have yet to EVER bargain in good faith. From Oslo to 2000 alone, they did more than 10,000 attacks on the innocent. There are Palestinian victims, but they are victimized by Hamas, not Israel. They are used as human shields and indoctrinated to believe that Israel must be destroyed.

1937 – Peel Commission. Offered a -two state solution. Palestinians were offered 96% of the West Bank. They said NO.

1947 – UN Partition Plan. Israel establishes itself as a state. Palestinians say NO to becoming its own state.

1967 – Israel took over the West Bank to provide a barrier to stop the missile attacks. Palestinians still said NO to becoming a state.

1993 – Oslo Accords. Israel gave land to Palestinians to help establish a two state solution and help the Palestinians to set up a government. They said NO.

1996 – PLO declares it wants to eliminate Israel.

2000 – Israel again offers 96% of the West Bank, PLO once again, NO.

2005 – Israel withdraws 8500 from the West Bank. Palestinians launched over 946 attacks on Israel and kills hundreds.

2008 – Israel offers 100% of the West Bank to the Palestinians, again, they say, NO.

Why so much anti-Semitism?

The plight of the "Palestinian People" is a manufactured crisis that the Arab world has encouraged and exploited for 50 years as a way to weaken Israel and limit Western influence in the Mid-East.

The Arab nations are not after peace. They are after the annihilation of Israel.

Muhammad himself declared 'the last hour will not come before the Muslims fight the Jews and the Muslims kill them.'

Muslims believe the 21st century to be the 'century of Islam' and that the annihilation of Israel is simply the **precursor to conquest in the West.**

The war in the Middle East is not about land, it is about religion. Their intention is still the same as that penned 3000 years ago.

Psalms 83: 2-4
2 For, lo, thine enemies make a tumult: and they that hate thee have lifted up the head.

 3 They have taken crafty counsel against thy people, and consulted against thy hidden ones.

 4 They have said, Come, and let us cut them off from being a nation; that the name of Israel may be no more in remembrance.

The gospel represents "freedom". It represents freedom from sin, freedom to make choices, freedom to live peaceably; freedom for man to govern himself.

It is a political and spiritual concept intertwined.
In the pre-mortal world we fought the battle against Lucifer for agency – the freedom to choose good or evil.

Today, if Satan is to stop freedom from spreading around the world, he must stop Israel and he must stop the gospel of Jesus Christ.

Israel represents freedom in the Old Testament region of the world, and is the only democracy in that region; and Satan must stop Christianity from spreading to the rest of the world, particularly those who have the priesthood and can offer freedom to those who are on the other side of the veil.

We fought Lucifer once and won. We will fight him and win again. We must not abandon our friends of Jewish heritage, the Israelites. We must defend what they represent to the world – freedom. We must defend America and what she represents to the world – freedom.

Prophecies and Commentaries

Using these books, I have made commentary about a possible timeline:

Book List:

Old and New Testament	Book of Mormon
George A. Smith Vision (internet)	John Taylor Vision (internet)
Charles Evans Vision (internet)	Cardston Prophecy (internet)
Visions of Glory, Pontius	Dream of Plagues, (internet)
Dreams and Visions, I, II, III, Young & Parrett	A Greater Tomorrow, Julie Rowe
George Washington Vision (internet)	Mosiah Hancock Vision (internet)
Cleansing of America, Skousen	There is No Death, Sarah Menet
Through the Window of Life, S. Freeman	Bishop Koyle (Dream Mine)
65 Signs of the Times. Ridges	Four Blood Moons, Pastor Hagee
The Mystery of the Shemitah	As A Thief in the Night, Roger Young
Whence Came They (10 Tribes)	The Last Days I & II, Young & Parrett

Signs that the End Times are NOW.

Gospel has been restored.
Gospel has been taken to the earth. (Internet fulfilled that prophecy.) Hastening is now.

Elijah restores the sealing keys.

First time Jews have possession of Jerusalem (1967). The Jews had possession of Israel in 1948, but not Jerusalem. Jews have found an unspotted heifer for their sacrifice. Jews have drawn up the temple plans to rebuild the temple. Jews base calendar on the moon. A tetrad is 4 blood moons together. Only 8 tetrads since Christ's birth. Every time the tetrad came on Jewish holidays and during the most significant events in their history. The next tetrad is 500 years from now.
http://2fletchdr222.blogspot.com/2014/04/the-history-of-8-blood-moon-tetrads.html
Four Blood Moons, Pastor John Hagee
The Mystery of the Shemitah, Jonathan Cahn
Isaiah Decoded, Avraham Gileadi

Jerusalem "cup of trembling" to those who attempt to fight her. Zechariah 12:2

Genealogical research expands. This is a spiritual war on both sides of the veil. Malachi 4:5-6

Lamanites blossom as a rose.
D&C 49:22-24 51% of the church is now outside of the U.S. 50% of the church speaks Spanish.

Knowledge explosion. (Phone, cars, machinery, electricity, internet, satellite, surgeries, etc.)
Daniel 12:4

Ecological damage occurs. (BP oil spill, Fukashima still pouring nuclear waste, over 70 tons into the ocean. Revelations 8:7-12

Doom and Gloom and Despair. D&C 1:35, Luke 21:25-27

Much selfishness and lack of caring. Hearts wax cold. Matthew 24:12

Wars and rumors of wars: **Do not be troubled, just the beginning or sorrows**. Matthew 24:6

Lawlessness and disrespect for authority. Chaos and revolutions. 2Nephi 28:20 D&C 45:26

Sexual immorality. 2Timoth 3:1, 6 Romans 1:24-31

Spirit stops working with the wicked. D&C 63:32 Pours out spirit on Saints Joel 2:29

Peace will be taken from the land. D&C 1:35

False prophets and churches abound. Joseph Smith - Matthew 1:22 Revelation 13:13-15

People refuse to believe obvious truth. 2Peter 3:3-4

People refuse to believe the signs of the times. 2Timothy 3:3-4

The Lord will come as a "thief in the night" to those who discount it is here. 1Thes 5:2, 2Peter 3:10

Signs and wonders on earth and in heaven. Four blood moons (tetrad), Climate changes, Solar flares, comets. D&C 45:36-40
http://www.foxnews.com/science/2014/10/21/earth-magnetic-field-could-flip-in-our-lifetime/

Many temples will be built. Isaiah 2:2 D&C 133:13

Famine - (CA feeds 25% of the world. Worst drought in history. Whole lakes gone. Rationing starting. No end in sight. TX started 3 years prior. Multiple fires from dry land. Cannot afford the water to be trucked in to plant.) Matthew 24:7   Sarah Menet, Temple Dreamer, Suzanne Freeman.

Climate change. (North and South Poles are splitting. 2014 NASA report.) Airports are 10 degrees off on radar, http://www.nasa.gov/topics/earth/features/2012-poleReversal.html

Earthquakes and other natural disasters. (EQ frequency has doubled in the last decade.) The Lord will begin his cleansing in his own house first. Utah will have an EQ and Plague at the same time on the heels of a worldwide financial collapse.   D&C 88:88-91, D&C 45:33,

D&C 112:24-26, Revelation 16:18, Revelation 6:12,
Sarah Menet, Spencer, Suzanne Freeman, Gayle Smith, Bishop Koyle all say there is a Utah EQ.
See events table and patterns.

Destroying angel will be allowed to go forth. D&C 8:5-8,

First "call out" (gathering) will take place to survive the plague. (Late spring.) Saints with food storage invited to go. Cars/trucks are available to haul preps. Less than 10% of the members go. Various reasons (don't grasp the urgency, don't want to share, don't want to leave possessions, etc.) Multiple visions.

Long winter is unusual and stops planting of crops, a great hailstorm destroys the crops, both add to the famine. D&C 29:16 Revelation 16:21
Multiple dreamers saw the long, harsh winter. Cleansing of America, p. 18, Joseph Smith talks about the great desolation of an earthquake, hail, famine and war that "will make an end to all nations".

Woe #1 (5 mo. War – Desert Storm, aggravated Middle East) Only 5 month war in recorded history. Description matches the events.

Woe #2 (13 mo. War and plague kill 3 billion on earth.) Read Charles Evans Dream about a civil war in America. See John Taylor's Dream about a plague (Ebola symptoms) that devastates the US and the World. See Sarah Menet, Suzanne Freeman, Spencer (VOG), Gayle Smith all see more than one plague killing the masses.

This is the "Abomination of Desolation" as spoken of by Daniel. The Savior is speaking to his disciples about an event from 200 years before him that was an abomination. He says the abomination will happen again (anti-christ will force them to worship an idol in their temple and Israel will be under seige), at which time they should stand in holy places and flee to the mountains. Revelation 13:14 Matthew 24:15-16

Multiple plagues at once.
See John Taylor's dream, See Dream of Plagues, See Sarah Menet.

Dollar Collapse. Worldwide depression begins. No work, no gas, no travel. Patriarch Charles Evans vision describes this in detail. Civil War in America ensues. Race rioting on a vast scale. See Cardston Prophecy. See Bishop Koyle vision. See Sarah Menet, Julie Rowe and Suzanne Freeman dreams. See George Albert Smith vision "collapse will make the great depression look like a picnic". See Astronomical Odds patterns of collapses.

When the dollar is collapsed intentionally by New World Order operatives such as Illuminati, Builderberg Group, UN Agenda 21, this will trigger a civil war for 13 months. The New World

Order calls for the earth's population to be reduced to 500,000 (See Agenda 21 on the UN website.) We are currently at 8 billion.

Tens of thousands (one family per acre) will come to Utah for peace, food, and safety (after the earthquake).

After the cleansing, thousands will receive calls to trek back to Missouri. Others will prepare and see Christ from where ever they are living. See Visions of Glory, see Through the Window of Life.

After 1.8 years in the mountains (call out), the men will come down to drive the foreign troops out of the land with the help of the Lost Tribes and re-establish the constitution. See George Washington vision, see White Horse Prophecy. See Visions of Glory. See Through the Window of Life.

Meeting at Adom-ondi-Ahman. Adam turns the keys of the priesthood back to Jesus Christ. The church prepares for the second coming of the Savior and to usher in the Millennium.

Famine is in full force. Mark of the Beast is instituted. No buying or selling without the chip in your hand. To receive the chip, you must denounce Jesus Christ or else be beheaded. Anti-Christ is at the helm over all nations. Suzanne Freeman, VOG, Sarah Menet, Revelation 13:1-8, 16-18

Israel builds a temple. See notes above on Israel/Jewish people.

Armageddon begins. Revelation 16:14-16

(3 year war – 3rd woe.) Revelation 11:14, Zechariah 11 to 14.

Two prophets killed. Revelation chapter 11.

Mt. of Olives split open. Zechariah 14:1-5

Christ rescues the Jews and teaches them the gospel.

Christ kills the world's army who went against the Jews.

Christ goes to Adam-ondi-Ahman. New Jerusalem is in the process of being built.   D&C 107:53-57, D&C 116, Daniel 7:9-14

Saints begin their trek back to Jackson County, MO. (takes years) **Mighty miracles occur.** Some get new transfigured bodies to complete this journey. People are raised from the dead. The plague is held back from the saints. A cloak of invisibility is provided for those in tent cities so the troops cannot find them.

VOG, Through the Windows of Life, Dream of Plagues,

This is the time to become "refined" enough to meet the Savior. We must abdicate all physical possessions, we must love and share under intense stress. We must rely on God for our every need. We must develop humility and patience before we can qualify to be in the presence of God. Thus, our journey, by foot back to MO. - Through the Windows of Life, Suzanne Freeman.

The Savior comes in from the heavens. The righteous are waiting (LDS and nonLDS) in MO and are lifted up to meet him. This includes those who are resurrected in the morning of the 1st resurrection.

The earth burns to stubble to take out any wicked who are left.

The Millennium is ushered in. Satan is bound for 1,000 years. Satan is release for a small season at the end of the 1,000 years for one final test and then he is bound forever.

Temples are open 24/7 for 1,000 years as people prepare for the final judgment, reconnect family lines, and work on spiritual progression.

Final judgment takes place. The souls who did not come forth in the first resurrection, come forth now.

Assignments are made to the three degrees of glory.

Visions Section

Church Archives

- **Patriarch Charles Evans**
- **President John Taylor**
- **Bishop John Koyle**
- **Heber C. Kimball**
- **President George Albert Smith**
- **Dream of Plagues**
- **Cardston Prophecy**
- **Joseph Smith**
- **White Horse Prophecy**

Visions from Church Members

- **Alma Erickson**
- **Moses Thatcher**
- **Sarah Menet (see www.nofearpreps.com)**
- **Julie Rowe (see www.nofearpreps.com)**
- **M. Sirrine**

Visions from Non LDS:

- **George Washington**

Charles D. Evans, Patriarch, Dream of Last Days

This is a dream from a volume at BYU Special Collections. This dream was included in The Contributor, Young Men's Mutual Improvement Association of the Latter-day Saints published in 1894 by The Deseret News Publishing Company.

While I lay pondering, in deep solitude, on the events of the present my mind was drawn into a reverie such as I had never felt before. A strong solitude for my imperiled country utterly excluded every other thought and raised my feelings to a point of intensity I did not think it possible to endure. While in this solemn, profound and painful reverie of mind, to my infinite surprise, a light appeared in my room, which seemed to be soft and silvery as that diffused from a northern star. At the moment of its appearance the acute feeling I had experienced instantly yielded to one of calm tranquility.

Although it may have been at the hour of midnight, and the side of the globe whereon I was situated, was excluded from the sunlight, yet all was light and bright and warm as an Italian landscape at noon; but the heat was softer or more subdued. As I gazed upward, I saw descending through my bedroom roof, with a gently gliding movement, a personage clothed in white apparel, whose countenance was smoothly serene, his features regular, and the flashes of his eye seemed to shoot forth scintillations, to use an earthly comparison, strongly resembling those reflected from a diamond under an intensely illuminated electric light, which dazzled but did not bewilder. Those large, deep, inscrutable eyes were presently fixed upon mine, when instantly placing his hands upon my forehead his touch produced an indescribable serenity and calmness, a calmness not born of earth, but at once peaceful, delightful and heavenly. My whole being was imbued with a joy unspeakable. All feelings of sorrow instantly vanished. Those lines and shadows which care and sorrow impress upon us were dispelled as a deep fog before a blazing sun. In the eyes of my heavenly visitor, for such he appeared to me, there was a sort of lofty pity and tenderness infinitely stronger than any such feeling I ever saw manifested in ordinary mortals. His very calm appeared like a vast ocean stillness, at once overpowering to every agitated emotion.

Son, I perceive thou hast grave anxieties over the perilous state of thy country, that thy soul has felt deep sorrow for its future. I have therefore come to thy relief and to tell thee of the causes that have led to this peril. Hear me attentively. Seventy-one years ago, after an awful apostasy of centuries, in which all nations were shrouded in spiritual darkness, when angels had withdrawn themselves, the voice of prophets hushed, and the light of Urim and Thummim shone not, and the vision of the seers was closed, while heaven itself shed not a ray of gladness to lighten a dark world, when Babel ruled and Satan laughed, and church and priesthood had taken their upward flight, and the voice of nations, possessing the books of the Jewish prophets, had ruled against vision and against Urim, against the further visits of angels, and against the doctrine of a church of apostles and prophets, thou knowest that then appeared a mighty angel with the solemn announcement of the hour of judgment, the burden of whose instructions pointed to dire calamities upon the present generation. This, therefore, is the cause of what thou seest and the end of the wicked hasteneth."

My vision now became extended in a marvelous manner, and the import of the past labors of the Elders was made plain to me. I saw multitudes fleeing to the place of safety in our mountain heights. The church was established in the wilderness. Simultaneously the nation had reached an unparalled prosperity, wealth unbounded, new territory was acquired, commerce extended, finance strengthened, confidence was maintained, and peoples abroad pointed to her as the model nation, the ideal of the past realized and perfected, the embodiment of the liberty sung by poets, and sought for by sages.

"But," continued the messenger, Thou beholdest a change. Confidence is lost. Wealth is arrayed against labor, labor against wealth, yet the land abounds with plenty for food and raiment, and silver and gold are in abundance. Thou seest also that letters written by a Jew have wrought great confusion in the finances of the nation which, together with the policy of many wealthy ones, has produced distress and do presage further sorrow."

Factions now sprang up as if by magic; capital had entrenched itself against labor throughout the land; labor was organized against capital. The voice of the wise sought to tranquilize these two powerful factors in vain. Excited multitudes ran wildly about; strikes increased; lawlessness sought the place of regular government. At this juncture I saw a banner floating in air whereon was written the words Bankruptcy, Famine, Floods, Fire, Cyclones, Blood, Plague. Mad with rage men and women rushed upon each other. Blood flowed down the streets of cities like water. The demon of bloody hate had enthroned itself on the citadel of reason; the thirst for blood was intenser than that of the parched tongue for water. Thousands of bodies lay untombed in the streets. Men and women fell dead from the terror inspired from fear. Rest was but the precursor of the bloody work of the morrow. All around lay the mournfulness of a past in ruins. Monuments erected to perpetuate the names of the noble and brave were ruthlessly destroyed by combustibles. A voice now sounded aloud these words, Yet once again I shake not the earth only, but also heaven. And this word yet once again signifies the removing of things that are shaken, as of things that are made; that those things that cannot be shaken may remain."

Earthquakes rent the earth in vast chasms, which engulfed multitudes; terrible groanings and wailings filled the air; the shrieks of the suffering were indescribably awful. Water wildly rushed in from the tumultuous ocean whose very roaring under the mad rage of the fierce cyclone, was unendurable to the ear. Cities were swept away in an instant, missiles were hurled through the atmosphere at a terrible velocity and people were carried upward only to descend in unrecognized mass. Islands appeared where ocean waves once tossed the gigantic steamer. In other parts voluminous flames, emanating from vast fires, rolled with fearful velocity destroying life and property in their destructive course. The seal of the dread menace of despair was stamped on every healing visage; men fell exhausted, appalled and trembling. Every element of agitated nature seemed a demon of wrathful fury. Dense clouds, blacker than midnight darkness, whose thunders reverberated with intonations which shook the earth, obscured the sunlight. Darkness reined, unrivalled and supreme.

Again the light shone, revealing an atmosphere tinged with a leaden hue, which was the precursor of an unparalleled plague whose first symptoms were recognized by a purple spot which appeared on the cheek, or on the back of the hand, and which, invariably, enlarged until it spread over the entire surface of the body, producing certain death. Mothers, on sight of it, cast away their children as though they were poisonous reptiles. This plague, in grown persons, rotted the eyes in their sockets and consumed the tongue as would a powerful acid or an intense heat. Wicked men, suffering under its writhing agonies, cursed God and died, as they stood on their feet, and the birds of prey feasted on their carcasses.

I saw in my dream the messenger again appear with a vile in his right hand, who addressing me said: Thou knowest somewhat of the chemistry taught in the schools of human learning, behold now a chemistry sufficiently powerful to change the waters of the sea."

He then poured out his vile upon the sea and it became putrid as the blood of a dead man, and every living soul therein died. Other plagues followed I forbear to record. A foreign power had invaded the

51

nation which, from every human indication, it appeared would seize the government and supplant it with monarchy. I stood trembling at the aspect, when, lo, a power arose in the west which declared itself in favor of the constitution in its original form; to this suddenly rising power every lover of constitutional rights and liberties throughout the nation gave hearty support. This struggle was fiercely contested, but the stars and stripes floated in the breeze, and, bidding defiance to opposition, waved proudly over the land. Among the many banners I saw, was one inscribed thus: The government based on the constitution, now and forever;" on another Liberty of Conscience, social, religious, and political."

The light of the gospel which had but dimly shown because of abomination, now burst forth with a luster that filled the earth. Cities appeared in every direction, one of which, in the center of the continent, was an embodiment of architectural science after the pattern of eternal perfections, whose towers glittered with a radiance emanating from the sparkling of emeralds, rubies, diamonds and other precious stones set in a canopy of gold and so elaborately and skillfully arranged as to shed forth a brilliancy which dazzled and enchanted the eye, excited admiration and developed a taste for the beautiful, beyond anything man had ever conceived. Fountains of crystal water shot upward their transparent jets which in the brilliant sunshine, formed ten thousand rainbow tints at once delightful to the eye. Gardens, the perfections of whose arrangement confound all our present attempts at genius, bedecked with flowers of varied hue to develop and refine the taste, and strengthen the love for these nature's chastest adornments. Schools and universities were erected, to which all had access; in the latter Urims were placed, for the study of the past, present and future, and for obtaining a knowledge of the heavenly bodies, and of the constructions of worlds and universes. The inherent properties of matter, its arrangements, laws, mutual relations were revealed and taught and made plain as the primer lesson of a child. The conflicting theories of geologists regarding the formation and age of the earth were settled forever. All learning was based on eternal certainty. Angels brought forth the treasures of knowledge which had lain hid in the womb of the dumb and distant past.

The appliances for making learning easy surpass all conjecture. Chemistry was rendered extremely simple, by the power which the Urims conferred on man of looking into and through the elements of every kind; a stone furnished no more obstruction to human vision than the air itself. Not only were the elements and all their changes and transformations plainly understood but the construction, operations, and laws of mind were thus rendered equally plain as those which governed the coarser elements. While looking through the Urim and Thummim I was amazed at a transformation, which even now is to me marvelous beyond description, clearly showing the manner in which particles composing the inorganic kingdom of nature are conducted upward to become a part of organic forms; another astounding revelation was a view clearly shown me of the entire circulation of the blood both in man and animals. After seeing these things and gazing once more upon the beautiful city, the following passage of Scripture sounded in my ears: Out of Zion the perfection of beauty God shineth."

On this I awoke to find all a dream.

I have written the foregoing, which is founded on true principle, under the caption of a dream, partly to instruct and partly to check the folly of reading silly novels now so prevalent.

Charles D. Evans
Springville, Utah.

John Taylor's Last Days Vision

by John Taylor (Source: Wilford Woodruff's Journal, June 15, 1878, "A Vision, Salt Lake City, Night of Dec 16, 1877")

NOTE: There are some that dispute whether or not it was John Taylor that had this vision. The vision does, in fact, come from the journal of Wilford Woodruff. It is verified that it was not Wilford Woodruff that had the vision. Many believe it to be John Taylor's vision.

I went to bed as usual at about 7:30PM. I had been read-ing a revela-tion in the French lan-guage. My mind was calm, more so than usual if possible, so I composed myself for sleep, but could not. I felt a strange feeling come over me and apparently be-came partially uncon-scious. Still I was not asleep, nor ex-actly awake, with dreary feeling. The first thing that I recognized was that I was in the tabernacle of Ogden, Utah. I was sit-ting in the back part of the build-ing for fear they would call on me to preach, which however they did, for after sing-ing the second time they called me to the stand.

I arose to speak and said that I did-n't know that I had anything es-pecially to say, ex-cept to bear my tes-timony of the Latter-day work, when all at once it seemed as if I was lifted out of myself and I said, "Yes, I have something to say and that is this: Some of my brethren have been ask-ing, "What is be-coming of us? What is the wind blowing?" I will answer you right here what is coming very shortly."

I was then in a dream, im-mediately in the city of Salt Lake, and wandering around in the streets and in all parts of the city, and on the doors of the houses I found badges of mourn-ing and I could not find a house but was in mourning. I passed my own house and found the same sign there, and I asked the ques-tion, "Is that me that is dead?" Someone gave me the an-swer, "No, you will get through it all."

It seemed strange to me that I saw no person in the streets in all my wan-dering around the coun-try. I seemed to be in their houses with the sick, but saw no funeral proces-sion, nor anything of the kind, but the city looking still and as though the people were praying. And it seemed that they had controlled the dis-ease, but what the dis-ease was I did not learn; it was not made known to me. I then looked over the country, north, east, south, and west, and the same mourning was in every land and in every place.

The next thing I knew I was just this side of Omaha. It seemed though I was above the earth, and look-ing down upon it. As I passed along upon my way east I saw the road full of people, mostly women, with just what they could carry in bundles on their backs, trav-eling to the moun-tains on foot. I won-dered how they would get through with such a small pack on their backs. It was re-markable to us[?] that there were so few men among them. It didn't seem to me as though the cars were run-ning, the rails looked rusty and the roads aban-doned; and I have no con-ception of how I traveled as I looked down upon the peo-ple.

I continued east by the way of Omaha and Council Bluffs, which were full of disease. There were women every-where. The state of Illinois and Mis-souri were in a tumult, men killing one an-other, women joining the fight-ing, fam-ily against family in the most horrid manner.

I imagined next that I was in Wash-ington and I found desola-tion there. The White House was empty and the Halls of Congress the same, and everything in ru-ins. The people seemed to have left the city and left it to take care of itself.

I was in Baltimore. In the square where the Monument of 1812 stands in front of the Char-les Hotel. I saw dead piled up so as to fill the street square. I saw mothers cutting the throats of their own children for their blood. I saw them suck it from their throats to quench their own thirst and then lie down and die. The water of Che-sapeake Bay was stagnant, and the stench arising from it on ac-count of their throw-ing their bod-ies into it so terrible, that the very smell carried death with it. I saw no man ex-cept they were dead or dying in the streets and very few women. Those I saw were crazy and in an ugly condi-tion. Everywhere I went I beheld the same sights all over the city; it was terrible be-yond description to look upon.

I thought this must be the end; but no, I was seemingly in an instant in the city of Philadel-phia. There eve-rything was still. No living soul was there to greet me. It seemed the whole city was with-out any inhabi-tants. In the south of Chestnut Street and in fact everywhere I went, the putrefaction of the dead caused such a stench that it was impos-sible for any living thing to breathe, nor did I see any living thing in the city.

Next I found myself in Broadway, in the city of New York, and there it seemed the people had done the best they could to overcome the disease, but in wandering down Broad-way I saw the bodies of beautiful women lying, some dead and oth-ers in a dy-ing condition, on the sidewalks. I saw men come out of cellars and ravish the per-sons of some that were yet alive and then kill them and rob their bodies of all the valu-ables they had upon them. Then before they could get back to the cellar they would roll over a time or two and die in ag-ony. In some of the back streets I saw them kill some of their own offspring and eat their raw flesh, and in a few minutes die them-selves. Every-where I went I saw the same scene of horror and de-struction and death and rap-ine.

No car-riages, buggies, or cars were running; but death and de-struc-tion were every-where. Then I saw fire start and just at that moment a mighty East wind sprang up and car-ried the flames over the city and it burned until there was not a sin-gle building left standing there, even down to the waters edge. Wharves and shipping all seemed to burn and follow in common destruction where the "great city" was a short time ago. The stench from the bodies that were burn-ing was so great that it was carried a long dis-tance cross the Hudson Bay and carried death and destruction wherever it pene-trated. I cannot paint in words the horror that seemed to compass me about; it was beyond description of man.

I sup-posed this was the end; but it was not. I was given to understand the same horror was being en-acted all over the coun-try, east, west, north, and south. Few were left alive, still there were some.

Immediately after I seemed to be standing on the left bank of the Mis-souri River, opposite e the City of In-de-pendence, but there was no city. I saw the whole state of Missouri and Illi-nois and all of Iowa, a complete desert with no living being there. A short dis-tance from the river how-ever, I saw twelve men dressed in temple robes, stand-ing in a square or nearly so (and I under-stood it repre-sented the Twelve Gates of the New Jerusa-lem.) Their hands were uplifted in consecration of the ground and lay-ing the corner stone of the tem-ple. I saw myraids of an-gels hovering over them, and saw also an immense pil-lar of clouds over them and heard the angels singing the most heav-enly music. The words were "Now is estab-lished the King-dom of God and his Christ, which shall never more be thrown down."

I saw people com-ing from the river and from the desert places a long way off to help build the temple and it seemed that hosts of an-gels all helped to get material to build with and I saw some of them who wore temple clothes come and build the tem-ple and the city, and all the time I saw the great pillar of clouds hovering over the place.

Instantly, however, I found my-self again in the taber-nacle at Ogden. And yet, I could still see the building go on and I got quite animated in call-ing on the people in the tabernacle to listen to the beautiful music, for the an-gels were singing the same music I had heard be-fore. "Now is estab-lished the King-dom of God and his Christ, which shall never more be thrown down."

At this I seemed to stagger back from the pulpit and Brother Francis D. Richards and some others caught my arm and prevented me from falling. Then I fin-ished so abruptly. Still even then I had not fainted, but was simply ex-hausted.

Then I rolled over in bed and awoke just as the city clock was strik-ing twelve.

Vision by President George Albert Smith

Recorded by DAVID HUGHES HORNE, P. E. Chemical Engineer, 28 February 1989

Sometimes rare, traumatic or shocking events become emblazoned into one's memory. This paper documents such an event. In 1946 I witnessed a prophetic utterance made by George Albert Smith, the Prophet and President of the Church of Jesus Christ of Latter—day Saints from 1945 to 1951. I am a son of Dr. Lyman Merrill Horne and Myrtle Swainston Horne. My father was a g-grandson of George A. Smith, cousin of the Prophet Joseph and Counselor to Brigham Young. His grandson President George Albert Smith was dad's mother's first cousin. From 1944 until March 1947 we lived on the same block in the Yale Ward as George Albert Smith and frequently had contact with him. Many times he paused at our home while on his evening walk and talked with me as I worked in our front yard. My family visited him a few times at his home, and he visited my family at our home several times. He always showed pleasure when I met him and once told me what work the Lord had for me to do and what I must do to be prepared to do His work.

One day our father arranged for George Albert Smith to speak to us in a family time. The Prophet told us of a vision he had had. At least 11 elements of it have occurred, and the rest may occur soon. My record of his prophecy may be important, because it may not be officially recorded. Last year I visited the Church Historian's Library to read Pres Smith's journal to see what he had written about it but the staff knew nothing about it. I then discussed it with Leonard Arrington, former Church Historian, who said, "I have never heard of it." Even Arthur Haycock, his faithful secretary, did not know of it, but he did not work with Pres. Smith until July 1947.

We dressed up in our best clothes. I shined my shoes again and again. Our father was disappointed with a sister who went to a movie with her boy friend. Dad asked her to stay with her beau, who had finished his navy service in August 1946, and share the evening with the Lord's Prophet, but she would not. We were seated at the given time in the living room ready for the Prophet to arrive. Present were my father, mother, sister, Alice Merrill Horne II (age 17), my brother, Robert H. Horne (14), my twin, Jonathan H. Horne, and I (11). It was after dark, and we had difficulty making the front porch light work. It was cold in that room, and I was glad to wear a coat. Thus I think his visit was between Oct 1946 and January 1947. Thereafter we were preparing to move. President Smith said much more than what I remember exactly, but some of his statements were so impressive that I have a brilliant recollection of them.

When George Albert arrived we sang a verse of "We Thank Thee O God for a Prophet." He stood and talked without notes for some time about the importance of keeping the commandments, always giving a full tithe, and being a good example wherever we are. He told us he once was on a train, in Mexico, with no other Northern European descent individuals. He said that a man recognized him as a leader of the "Mormon" Church, and introduced himself as a Mexican government official. President Smith noted how embarrassed he and the Church would have been had he not been acting as a faithful servant of the Lord should. I also heard him tell that story in another talk.

Then President Smith said, "I have had a troublesome vision of another great and terrible war that made the war just ended look like a training exercise, and people died like flies. It began at a time when the Soviet Union's military might dwarfed that of the United States, and we, that is the United States, would have missiles that carried an atomic bomb in Europe. I saw the United States withdraw its missiles to appease the Soviet Union, and then the war began." He also said that we would have big missiles in deep holes he described like grain silos which the Soviets would try to destroy by their own missiles. They would hit military installations and some cities also. He said that the president at that time would be of Greek extraction.

Until then all the presidents would be of British or Northern European ancestry. He continued that the U.S. would be bound by numerous entangling alliances and would take away weapons owned by the people. He talked some about the initial attack and the ground warfare, but I can't remember enough to document all their tactics and in which countries various things occurred. One tactic, especially in Europe, was to transport tanks in thousands of big trucks like semi trailers on the super highways to have them located where they wanted them when the war was to begin. During that explanation I asked, "What about the Atomic Cannon?" to which he answered, "I didn't see anything like that." Then he said, "The aftermath was dreadful. Think of the worst, most difficult times of the depression." He turned to us children and said, "You won't remember the depression," which was true. I didn't know there was a depression as I was growing up; the sun came up every morning, flowers bloomed, we went to school, and there was church every Sunday. But he repeated to our parents, "Think of the worst condition of the depression. Can you think of something?" to which our father answered, "Oh yes!" Then President Smith continued, "You know how Sunday School picnics are complete with salad, chicken, root beer, and dessert, and everyone has a wonderful time. That worst time of the depression will seem like a Sunday School picnic when compared with how conditions will be after that great war." When he finished speaking, he turned around and went to the front door. As he left I thought to myself, "What he said is really important. I've got to remember it!"

To understand Pres. George Albert Smith's woeful statement, "I have had a troublesome vision..." one first must comprehend the kind of man President Smith was. Those who knew him best describe him as the most humble, compassionate, magnanimous, kind, and merciful person they knew. He exemplified the Pure Love of Christ and showed his love for all of God's children by his unqualified service. For example, at World War II's end he organized a relief program for war torn Europe's destitute people. The Relief Society sisters made quilts and clothes. The Church welfare cannery produced millions of cases of food donated from farms and home gardens. Other materials and food were purchased from donations by church members world wide. Then he obtained U.S. Pres. Truman's permission to send the aid and assigned Elder Ezra Taft Benson to administer its distribution in Europe. The aid was not restricted to L.D.S. Church members. The government of Greece honored Pres. Smith for his and the Church's service to its people. Thereafter the Government initiated The Marshall Plan, and organizations like CARE sprang up. Thus for him to see an event of which he also said in his April 1950 Conf concluding speech, "..people by the millions will die like flies," CR—4/50:5,l69 indeed must have been a troublesome vision (see also Harold B. Lee CR—l0/51:28—29).

When President Smith told us of his vision, the U.S. and the USSR were allies. Some tiffs had occurred between the USSR and the U.S., but the idea that the Soviets would become an enemy wasn't popular. In 1946 the USA was the world's great military power. It seems the allies of the

U.S. succeeded in World War II because we had sent them material. The idea that the USSR would dwarf the US's military might was contrary to any reasonable expectation, but today it is exactly true. The Soviet's military might is awesome. Nearly all their population including peasant farmers serve in their reserves and may become part of their army in time of war. They have amassed a year's supply of food (including U.S. grain) so they will not have to farm the first year of any war. They have about five times as many fighter and several times as many modern bomber aircraft as we do. They are well made, effective aircraft with well trained pilots and crews. Their infantry's weapons and logistics preparations are staggering. Thus, two elements of Pres. Smith's vision were exactly correct; the USSR became our enemy, and their military might dwarfs our own.

It's no secret we have nuclear warhead missiles in Europe and underground silos here But in 1946 nuclear missiles were beyond imagination. Even Massachusetts Institute of Technology's president in 1950 said, "Intercontinental ballistic missiles with nuclear warheads are impossible." But we had them by 1963; I've worked in Minuteman Missile silos which accurately fit Pres. Smith's description. But our cruise missiles were made after 1980. General Bernard Rogers, NATO Commander, was so outspoken against the INF treaty that he was removed. General John Gavins, his successor, said that he could not maintain Europe in a war for more than two weeks without nuclear weapons. So five more elements of Pres Smith's vision are verified; we have missiles, in Europe, and in silos, that carry atomic bombs, and are essential for U.S. defense.

Next President Smith said that we would withdraw our missiles from Europe to appease the Soviets. Former UN Ambassador Jean Kirkpatrick said that the INF treaty hurts us militarily, but we have to do it. Dr. Eugene Callens says the treaty was politically motivated, missiles were used as bargaining chips in negotiations with the Soviets, which is a form of appeasement, and Pres. Reagan may have been buying time with their removal until other new systems were in place. During the negotiations we revealed we knew the USSR plans to violate the treaty. Thus two more elements of Pres. Smith's vision are verified; on 1 Sept 88 the U.S. began removing missiles to comply with a treaty designed to appease the Soviets. By 31 Dec 89 our missiles should be disarmed.

Just before Pres. Smith visited us, the newspaper headlined a giant, about 24 wheel, artillery piece named the Atomic Cannon. It was to have been like Big Bertha Germany used to batter Liege, Namur and Paris. The Atomic Cannon was designed to fire atomic bombs 100—miles to assure no potential aggressor ever would start another war. But Pres. Smith said he did not see anything like that. History reveals the Atomic Cannon was a flop, and by about 1948 the program was canceled. The U.S. has a howitzer able to fire a nuclear weapon about 20 miles, but it is very different from the colossus shown in the news. Thus another element of Pres. Smith's prophecy is verified.

As predicted, all U.S. presidents have had North European or British ancestry. But in 1988 a man of Greek descent led the polls for a time. He may run again. Thus one more element of Pres. Smith's vision is realized; we see how another element could occur.
The next elements in President Smith's prophecy were another great and terrible war, it would make World War II look like a training exercise, and people would die like flies. This obviously hasn't happened, but consider some of the Soviets' weapons and military preparations and the

results of their use. The Soviets have 100—megaton hydrogen bombs which could be used against military bases and cities. Also, when the Soviets tested one of their first 100—megaton bombs the Electromagnetic Pulse (EMP), which is an incredibly high energy radio wave produced by the detonation, melted an electrical system power transformer's windings 190—miles away. The Soviets are far ahead of the U.S. in space technology and the number of satellites in orbit. From January through September 1987 the Soviets fired more than 700 vehicles into space, mostly military. The U.S. space program for that same time was almost stopped. And some military analysts believe some of the Soviet satellites in orbit above the U.S. contain high yield nuclear bombs purposefully to destroy the all transformers in the nationwide power grid, computers, radios, TVs, telephones and most other electronic devices in the U.S. Pacemakers and electronic watches may be blown out, too. Most transistors, diodes, integrated circuits and other semiconductor devices can tolerate less than 30—volts, but EMP is about a 50,000 volt/meter wave. Evacuation from cities before the bombs hit may be difficult, because new vehicle engines and alternators today have semiconductor controls. Their junctions could be melted in a millionth of a second by the EMP. It may be as if for an instant the entire continent Were a microwave oven. Older vehicles with points in their distributors and mechanical voltage regulators may continue to operate if their alternator diodes are not blown. Diodes and electronic auto parts can be replaced if spares exist that were shielded. Amateur radio gear with electron tubes still may work afterward. But well pumps that supply our drinking water may be out of service for a long time.

The USSR's military buildup is not to protect their country from invasion. Who since Hitler has invaded the USSR? Instead, the USSR has been the aggressor in many wars throughout the world. Two reliable military sources have told me that on 4 July 1987 a Soviet Bear bomber 2,000 miles from Hawaii fired an intermediate range missile at Hawaii. When it was about 100 miles from Honolulu the U.S. had not destroyed it, and a Soviet aircraft that was there shot it down. The military information officer reported that when he revealed the story to the news media the media managers refused to air it saying, "It would be bad for business." Recent reports of Soviet landings on the Aleutian Islands and other places suggest they are practicing for an Invasion.

If the war Pres Smith saw occurs, conditions will be like our pre—1800 ancestors knew with some shelters but few modern machines by which we work. Conditions will be worse for a long time. Government and major services including police; electricity; potable water & waste; fuel; and commercial food, medicines, & clothes may not exist. Engines to power pumps, vehicles and machines may not work; 3 Nephi 21:14—15 says that if the gentiles don't repent the Lord will destroy their chariots, cities, and strongholds. Our ancestors had wagons and horses for transportation and work. Shovels, hoes, seed, and bikes with puncture resistant tubes may be scarce. There may be no food from farms other than what will be carried, no manufactured goods, or any safe drinking water. Our forbearers knew how to do things without our machines that we do not know how to do. Thus, conditions could be exactly like Pres. Smith described; the worst conditions of the depression would seem like a Sunday School picnic in comparison.

In about 1940 my parents started a Sunday evening study group which their friend Dr. Sidney B. Sperry taught. In about 1964 while studying the Doctrine and Covenants Dr. Sperry noted Sect 1:17 said a calamity would come upon the children of men. He told us of an experience he had with Pres. George Albert Smith at the end of a conference. Dr. Sperry said, "I rushed up onto the platform to speak with Pres. Smith after the prayer. When I arrived at his side he was standing, overlooking the congregation. The people were just starting to stand up, and the ushers were just starting to open the doors so they could leave. And I heard the President woefully mutter as he looked over the congregation... They"ll die like flies."" Dr. Sperry explained his concern that Pres. Smith looked at the Saints and said, "They'll die like flies," Neither my father, mother nor I said anything to the group what Pres Smith told us in our home. Knowing Pres. Smith considered Saints would be among those whom he told us would die like flies greatly concerns me, too. For I am one of them and was in the Tabernacle when that occurred. I went to conference in the Tabernacle when I was young and saw Dr. Sperry rush up to the speakers' platform at the end of a conference. Perhaps I feel like Laman felt about the Jews at Jerusalem being righteous- that many Saints are honorable, diligent in the Lord's work, and doers of the word, not hearers only. Yet I know Pres. Benson has said that the revelation on the production and storage of food may be as important to our temporal salvation as it was for Noah to get into the ark. And few have complied with this Counsel of the Lord's Living Prophet.

Remember the Lord said, "If ye are prepared ye shall not fear." Ancient prophets knew our day would be difficult yet yearned to see it. The Saints are commanded to obey & teach the Lord's laws; to multiply and fill the earth; and build the Lord's Kingdom. Our task is not to shrink but to prepare for challenges that may demand our greatest efforts to survive free from AIDS or plagues that otherwise might infect everyone.

I record this as a witness of my friend and cousin, George Albert Smith's description of a prophetic vision he saw. I began writing it last Sept and have remembered more as I concentrated on his comments. I've not recorded here all I now remember. See also Pres. Smith's General Conference speeches CR-1O/46:149-153 & CR-10/50:180-181.

After reading my 28 Oct version my brother Robert said he remembered Pres. Smith's visit exactly as I wrote it but doesn't remember some I since added. Alice said she remembered some of the 23 Dec version. On 18 Dec Dr. Hugh Nibley said his mother (a close friend of Pres. Smith) told him about the vision which Pres. Smith received at a conference in the Bay Area and related it in his talk. Dr. Nibley also said he was close to LeGrand Richard's family and Sister Richards told him about the vision, too.

Additional Statement of David Hughes Horne, P.E., copyrighted March 26, 1989

David Horne also mentioned that President Smith indicated that this nuclear attack would take place on a holiday after the new president was elected, but before he took office. The following war would involve many of the countries of the world but President Smith talked specifically about Europe, Germany, Hungary, Israel, Turkey, United States, and the Soviet Union, as well as a few others.
1.Statement of David Hughes Horne, P.E., copyrighted March 26, 1989

Heber C Kimball - 1931

An army of Elders will be sent to the four quarters of the earth to search out the righteous and warn the wicked of what is coming. All kinds of religions will be started and miracles performed that will deceive the very elect if that were possible. Our sons and daughters must live pure lives so as to be prepared for what is coming. After a while the Gentiles will gather by the thousands to this place, and Salt Lake City will be classed among the wicked cities of the world. A spirit of speculation and extravagance will take possession of the Saints, and the results will be financial bondage.

Persecution comes next and all true Latter-day Saints will be tested to the limit. Many will apostatize and others will be still not knowing what to do. Darkness will cover the earth and gross darkness the minds of the people. The judgments of God will be poured out on the wicked to the extent that our Elders from far and near will be called home, or in other words the gospel will be taken from the Gentiles and later on carried to the Jews.

The western boundary of the State of Missouri will be swept so clean of its inhabitants that as President Young tells us, when you return to that place, there will not be left so much as a yellow dog to wag his tail.

Before that day comes, however, the Saints will be put to a test that will try the integrity of the best of them. The pressure will become so great that the more righteous among them will cry unto the Lord day and night until deliverance comes.

Then the Prophet Joseph and others will make their appearance and those who have remained faithful will be selected to return to Jackson County, Missouri and take part in the building of that beautiful city, the New Jerusalem. (Heber C. Kimball, First Counselor in the First Presidency, May 1868, in Deseret News, 23 May 1931; see also Conference Report, Oct. 1930, p. 58-59)

JOSEPH SMITH

"The United States will spend her strength and means warring in foreign lands until the other nations will say, "Let us divide up the lands of the United States" . Then the people of the U.S. will unite and swear by the blood of their forefathers that the land shall not be divided. Then, the country will go to war, and they will fight until one half of the U.S. Army will give up, and the rest will continue to struggle. They will keep on until they are very ragged and discouraged, and almost ready to give up - when the Boys from the Mountains will rush forth in time to save the American Army from defeat and ruin. And they will say, "Brethren we are glad you have come; give us men, henceforth, who can talk with God." Then you will have friends, but you will save the country when its liberty hangs by a thread, as it were."

The Words of Joseph Smith Page 180-181

"Remarks on the coming of the Son of Man by Joseph Smith the Prophet, made in Nauvoo. Christ says no man knoweth the day or the hour when the Son of Man cometh. This is a sweeping argument for sectarianism against Latter day ism. Did Christ speak this as a general principle throughout all generations. Oh no, he spoke in the present tense, No man that was then living upon the footstool of God knew the day or the hour, But he did not say that there was no man throughout all generations that should not know the day or the hour. No, for this would be in flat contradiction with other scripture for the prophet says that God will do nothing but what he will reveal unto his Servants the prophets, consequently if it is not made known to the Prophets, it will not come to pass..."

THE WHITE HORSE PROPHECY

Some questions have arisen regarding the authenticity of the "White Horse Prophecy" because it was not documented at the time that it was to have been given. Edwin Rushton and Theodore Turley were witnesses to this prophecy and gave their testimony to its validity.

A few years before the death of Edwin Rushton in 1904, he was requested by several close friends to make a recorded and notarized statement regarding this prophecy. His friends James H. Anderson acted as recorder and Arnold G. Giauque was notary for the following account of this prophecy.
[49] On or about the 6th day of May, 1843, a grand review of the Nauvoo Legion was held in Nauvoo. The Prophet Joseph complimented them for their good discipline and evolutions performed. The weather being hot, he called for a glass of water. With the glass of water in his hand he said, "I drink to you a toast to the overthrow of the mobocrats."

The next morning a man who had heard the Prophet give the toast returned to visit the mansion of the Prophet, and so abused him with bad language, that the man was ordered out by the Prophet. It was while the two were out that my attention was attracted to them and hearing the man speaking in a loud tone of voice, I went toward them; the man finally leaving. There were present the Prophet Joseph Smith, Theodore Turley and myself. The Prophet began talking to us of the mobbings and drivings and persecutions we as a people have endured, but, said he, "We will have worse things to see; our persecutors will have all the mobbings they want. Don't wish them any harm, for when you see their sufferings you will shed bitter tears for them.

"While this conversation was going on, we stood by his south wicket gate in a triangle. Turning to me he said: "I want to tell you something. I will speak in a parable like unto John the Revelator. You will be in the Rocky Mountains, and you will be a great and mighty people established there, which I will call the White Horse of Peace and Safety." When the Prophet said you will see it, I asked him, "Where will you be at that time?" He said, "I shall never go there. Your enemies will continue to follow you with persecutions and will make obnoxious laws against you in Congress to destroy the White Horse, but you will have a friend to defend you to throw out the worst part of [50] the laws, so they will not hurt much. You must continue to petition Congress all the time, but they will not give you your rights but will govern you with strangers and commissioners; you will see the Constitution of the United States almost destroyed; it will hang by a thread, as it were, as fine as the finest silk fiber."

At this point, the Prophet's countenance became sad; he said, "I love the Constitution. It was made by the inspiration of God, and it will be preserved and saved by the efforts of the White Horse and the Red Horse, who will combine in its defense. The White Horse will raise an ensign on the tops of the mountains of peace and safety. The White Horse will find the mountains full of minerals and they will become very rich. You will see silver piled in the streets. You will see gold shoveled up like sand. Gold will be of little value even in a mercantile capacity, for the people of the world will have something else to do in seeking for salvation. The time will come when the banks in every nation will fail and only two places will be safe where people can deposit their gold and treasures. These places will be the White Horse and England's vaults.

A terrible revolution will take place in the land of America, such as has never been seen before; for the land will literally be left without a supreme government and every species of wickedness will run rampant. Father will be against son, and son against father, mother against daughter, and daughter against mother. The most terrible scenes of murder and bloodshed and rapine that have ever been looked upon will take place.

[51] Peace will be taken from the earth and there will be no peace only in the Rocky Mountains. This will cause many thousands of the honest in heart to gather there; not because they would be saints, but for safety and because they would not take up the sword against their neighbor.

You will be so numerous that you will be in danger of famine, but not for the want of seed time and harvest, but because of so many to be fed. Many will come with bundles under their arms to escape the calamities, and there will be no escape except by fleeing to Zion.

Those that come to you will try to keep the laws and be one with you, for they will see your unity and the greatness of your organization. The Turkish Empire will be one of the first powers to be disrupted, for freedom must be given for the Gospel to be preached in the Holy Land.

The Lord took the best blood of the nations and planted them on the small islands now called England and Great Britain, and gave them great power in the nations for a thousand years and their power will continue with them, that they might keep the balance of power and keep Russia from usurping her power over all the world. England and France are now bitter enemies, but they will be allied together and be united to keep Russia from conquering the world.

The two Popes, Greek and Catholic, will come together and be united. The Protestant religions do not know how much they are indebted to Henry the VIII for throwing off the Pope's Bull and establishing the Protestant faith. He was the only monarch who could do so at the time, and he did it because this [52] nation, England, was at his back to sustain him. One of the peculiar features of England is the established red coat, a uniform making so remarkable a mark to shoot at, and yet they have conquered wherever they have gone. The reason for this will be known by them some day. The Lion and the Unicorn of Israel is their ensign; the wisdom and statesmanship of England comes from having so much of the blood of Israel in the nation.

While the terrible revolution of which I have spoken has been going on, England will be neutral until it becomes so inhuman that she will interfere to stop the shedding of blood. England and France will unite together to make peace, not to subdue the nations; they will find the nations so broken up and so many claiming government, till there will be no responsible government. Then it will appear to the other nations as though England had taken possession of the country. The Black Horse will flee to the invaders and will join with them, for they have fear of becoming slaves again, knowing England did not believe in slavery, fleeing to them they believe would make them safe; armed with British bayonets, the doings of the black horse will be terrible." (Here the Prophet said he could not bear to look on the scene as shown him in vision and asked the Lord to close the scene.)

Continuing, he said, "During this time the great White Horse will have gathered strength sending out Elders to gather the honest in heart among the Pale Horse, or people of the United States, to stand by the Constitution of the United States, as it was given by inspiration of God."

[53] In these days God will set up a kingdom, never to be thrown down, for other kingdoms to come unto. And these kingdoms that will not let the gospel be preached will be humbled until they will. England, Germany, Norway, Denmark, Sweden, Switzerland, Holland and Belgium have a considerable amount of the blood of Israel among their people which must be gathered. These nations will submit to the Kingdom of God. England will be the last of these kingdoms to surrender; but when she does, she

will do it as a whole in comparison as she threw off the Catholic power. The nobility know that the gospel is true, but it has not enough pomp and grandeur and influence them to embrace it.

They are proud and will not acknowledge the kingdom of God, or come unto it until they see the power which it will have. Peace and safety in the Rocky Mountains will be protected by a cordon band of the White Horse and the Red Horse.

The coming of the Messiah among this people will be so natural that only those who see Him will know that He has come, but He will come and give His laws unto Zion, and minister unto His people. This will not be His coming in the clouds of Heaven to take vengeance on the wicked of the world.

The Temple in Jackson County will be built in this generation. The saints will think there is not time enough to build it; built with the help you will receive, you can put up a great temple quickly. They will have all the gold, silver, and precious stones; for these things only will be used for the beautifying of the temple; all the skilled mechanics you want, and the Ten Tribes of Israel will help you build it. When you see this land, bound with iron, you may look toward Jackson County.

[54] At this point, he made a pause, and looking up as though the vision was still in view, he said, "There is a land beyond the Rocky Mountains that will be invaded by the heathen Chinese unless great care and protection are given. Where there is no law, there is no condemnation, and this will apply to them (the heathen nations). Power will be given the White Horse to rebuke nations afar off, and they will be one with the White Horse, but when the law goes forth they will obey; for the law will go forth from Zion. The last great struggle Zion will have to contend with will be when the whole of the Americans will be made the Zion of our God. Those opposing will be called Gog and Magog (some of the nations of the world led by Russian czar) and their power will be great, but all the opposition will be overcome and then this land will be the Zion of our God."

The Vision of Alma Erickson (1930)

Vision of Alma Erickson (early 1930's)

The voice of warning crying unto me, concerning the great and dreadful day of the Lord and the destruction of the wicked, which shall shortly come to pass.

The voice of the Great Spirit does reveal these things unto me, even the Holy Ghost that does bear witness of the Father and the Son. Therefore, I call unto all to repent of their wrong doings and their wickedness, and join the Church of Jesus Christ of Latter-day Saints.

It is essential that ye be baptized in the name of the Father, and of the Son, and of the Holy Ghost, that ye may receive instructions and be taught the truth by the Spirits which are in Heaven.

Thus declareth the voice of the Great Spirit which is within me, even the Holy Ghost. For thus saith the Spirit unto me, it is your burden and responsibility that these things made manifest unto you shall be made known unto the world.

Prophesy unto this people, for their sins have come up unto me, and they are not of me. He, who will not hearken unto the Law of My Word, shall sink into unquenchable fire. Therefore, I extend a warning unto all who will hear the word of their Great Creator, to repent of their sins and evil doings, lest God's judgment come upon them and destruction overtake them.

All these things I make known unto you concerning the Great and Dreadful Day of the Lord, and the destruction of the wicked, which shall shortly come to pass, and is even now at our doors.

Behold, this people, they esteem one another according to their possession of wealth, and not according to the value of the soul. They look upon the wonders of the earth and marvel, but fail to see the poor people who suffer in want around them and among them.

The whole earth is now ripe for destruction, and it shall shortly and speedily come upon the inhabitants of the earth, for God shall hasten His work, and great destruction shall quickly overtake the evildoers, and who is there among them that can escape God's holy law and His chastening hand?

I see our church represented by a high building, and we are in the top thereof, or the most recently constructed portion, which is very shaky; and I perceive that this last constructed portion is going to fall, and we must get down to the lower part of this great structure, which rests solidly upon its foundations. And while I am thus viewing it, the top, or last part built, does crash with a loud and fearful crash.

I see sheep grazing in the valley and on the mountain side. My Master tells me to watch them and not let them graze too far away from camp, because the sky gathers blackness and a bad storm is drawing near. I call three times, and the last time they hear me and come swiftly toward camp.
And thus does declare the Holy Ghost unto me: Beware, lest ye be destroyed with the wicked, for these things shall shortly come to pass.

Poverty and starvation shall sweep the land, and there shall be large masses of destitute people, masses of humanity starving. And as a witness to this truth, you shall see large headlines in the newspapers declaring starvation and hunger; and pictures of masses of humanity but a short way off who are starving. I warn you all to look to God; call on the Mighty One, even your Heavenly Father. Keep His commandments and lay up supplies against this time.

Starvation shall sweep the country, and in certain places, people will even harvest cactus and prickly pears, and prepare food for themselves and to sell. And I see that food becomes so scarce that soldiers are stationed to guard the plates of those who are eating, that the hungry may not steal their food.

Because of the wickedness of this people, they are brought down into bondage, and their money which they have prized so highly, becomes increasingly worthless. I see the time when a cheap room in a hotel will cost $9.00. Then I see a law passed declaring U.S. money is of no value; and the rich bemoan the loss of their great piles of money. I see silver coins lying around in the dirt, and I look around and see still more of them, and in certain places, they are in piles on the dirt. Greenback bills become worthless scraps of paper, and have no value. And thus it shall be that U.S. money becomes worthless.

I see industries collapse. The gasoline and oil industry is symbolized to me by a great pipeline that extends out of the earth a mile or so into the sky, thence a mile to the north, and thence down to the earth. Then I see this great man-made structure is leaking badly at the south, and then it springs a leak at the north, and then it falls northward with a mighty crash.

Thus it shall come to pass that the gasoline and oil business shall first fail in the south, and it shall spread to the north, until there is a complete oil and gasoline failure. And none shall be hauled over the rails because of the great failure. Traffic and industries shall cease because of the want of oil and gas, and great consternation shall seize upon man.

And it shall come to pass that wickedness shall increase, and many women in general shall partake of whoredoms for hire, for women shall exceed the men in number. And I see many men turning to robbery, and to liquors and strong drink, and their children are deprived of the teachings of our Lord and Saviour, Jesus Christ.

The Lord God shall send forth flies extra early, and they shall attack the evil doers, the children of the devil, and fear shall fall upon the wicked, insomuch that they shall not move out of their places.

But the more righteous shall flee unto Zion. And I see large crowds coming to Utah in such great numbers that they have to be handled in masses, or in herds like cattle.

And again, I see this same fly as it is revealed to me by the Great Spirit. It is quite a large and fiery red or brass colored fly sent to attack the wicked

.. Pestilence shall spread from its bite, insomuch that the flesh shall fall from off the bones, and the eyes from the sockets, and the tongue shall not speak. I also saw a dog and a gray bitch wolf, and the wolf is exceedingly heavy with pups to be born. They shall increase in numbers, and shall be ravenously hungry, and they shall not hesitate to attack man; and because of their great numbers, they shall overpower and devour him. Man shall try to tame these beasts, but to no avail. Their purpose is to destroy.

And tornadoes shall come right here in our own west; and I see a dark colored rainbow appear in the Southern sky, followed by another great sign across the whole sky like a checkerboard, and the Lord God shall speak with a mighty voice of fierce and sweeping winds, and buildings, automobiles and people shall be swept away. And I see also that written words shall appear in the sky as a sign and a warning of great destruction.

High winds shall spread over the country with tornadoes and cyclones in various places. Houses shall be blown to pieces and some carried up into the air. The government will issue tents to the homeless. I see a great storm that shall come suddenly, sweeping up glass and causing it to rain down on many, causing much bloodshed. Fire and smoke shall spread over the land and many strange sights shall be seen.

The ocean shall become exceedingly rough in the winter months, and a fear shall arise in the hearts of the people for the safe return of their relatives and friends and those who must go to sea; for it becomes impossible to cross in the winter months, and all must cross by or before the last ship of the season, or wait until the next season when the ocean calms. And at this time, the ocean shall be out of its bounds, or regular water levels, and shall rise up and wash away many towns along the seashores. And afterwards, other people will come in and reinhabit these towns, bringing with them food that is not produced in the ocean-swept country. And I see the water mark on the side hills, high above the towns.

I look up above the eastern horizon and see a woman dressed in a white robe, which also encloses her head, excepting her face; and she is sitting at the foot of a great white cross, which has golden stars in it. As I look upon this scene, it moves toward the north, and I am told to write of great and bloody wars to come.

Again the vision of my mind is opened and I see two emblems through dark clouds; they are the emblem of the American Legion and the American flag. And as I look at them, they appear to be on a government building. They begin to fade away until they have completely vanished from my sight. I see only the government building without either of these emblems.

And I see a crowd of people looking at this great wonder in the sky, and they are somewhat afraid, but not enough that they repent of their wickedness. And I see one man make an effort to pray to the Lord when he sees this great sign, but he makes a failure or mockery out of it, and everyone at the gathering breaks up and leaves in confusion.

I see that the judgments of the Lord are poured out upon all flesh, and it is shown to me that this great sign and wonder marks the time when great signs and wonders shall appear in the sky; and this is the time when the wicked shall be destroyed.

Then I see the U.S. flag with all its bright colors in the northwestern sky; and then it disappears and another flag appears in its stead, which is plain and without colors; but made up of many different parts. And the meaning of it is made clear, that the people of the U.S. will disagree and divide up and split up, forming many separate organizations, until the central government is completely overthrown, and the nation is in civil chaos--without civil administration or leadership.

And it shall come to pass, that the French nation shall bomb the eastern seacoast of the U.S. with a deadly poison gas, and it shall spread over the land like a blanket of thick heavy smoke of a dirty white or a light yellow color; and it does spread over the land with wind and carries with it to all it touches.

A war shall come in this land, for I see a war in the west. I see a mighty gun that shoots from the mountains of the Lord toward the east, drops of rain, as it were, each drop carrying death wherever it hits. First a beam of light comes out of the west and extends across the sky towards the east, and then I see two lines of clouds come out of the west following along each side of the beam of light. And I see them in the east fortifying themselves against these raindrops of death.

Salt Lake County shall be colored red with many light snows, and northern lights shall come in these times, and be seen out of their regular bounds, and shall show in regions where they have never been seen before. And in that day, the sun shall lose its brightness, and darkness shall fall upon the face of the earth; but it shall come to pass that in certain places of the more righteous, the countryside shall be lighted by a miracle line unto a beautiful lamp in the sky, for it is the will of the Lord that certain crops of the righteous shall not fail, and the interior of rooms shall be lighted by a miracle, and even the inside of buildings and mines.

I see hay come down out of the sky like manna from heaven to feed hay-eating animals, and many haystacks of the righteous increase of themselves by the power of God.

But upon dense populations of the wicked, smoke and vapor and dampness and a dark cloud shall settle down and encompass their houses, and shall not rise. When these low clouds appear, there shall be lightning and explosions in the air, the worst that have ever been heard. I see these rapid swirling clouds moving swiftly close to the ground, causing great friction and noise; but to the west, they play out, and toward Utah the sky remains clear.

And thus it shall be when the Lord begins to hasten His work in the destruction of the wicked. There shall be a great sign and all shall see it, for low clouds shall be seen floating low to the ground.

And the Great Spirit or the Holy Ghost declared unto me, Alma Erickson, that the very time of these low clouds is the time appointed by the Lord when the wicked shall not stand. Therefore, know ye that when these low clouds shall come, the wicked of the earth shall be destroyed; and the sun shall lose its brightness, and the earth shall become cooler as a result; causing more clouds to form and come low to the ground, indicating the beginning of the Great and Dreadful Day of the Lord.

And I see these low clouds coming down over the hills and moving with the wind, causing intervals of dimmer sunshine and cooler temperatures. And I begin to hear thunderings and see tornadoes coming over the hills and across the valleys.

And when the temperatures of the earth have fallen because of the low clouds, people will be obliged to go into one room of their houses, and to huddle about their heater to keep warm, and cold and hunger shall come upon man, for this is the time when the wicked shall be destroyed from off the face of the earth.

The word of the Lord came to me, saying that books containing the word of our Heavenly Father and Savior and the Holy Ghost, shall be speedily transferred to Zion, just before the great and dreadful day of the Lord.

It is revealed to me by the Holy Ghost that in a deep narrow gorge, in a southeasterly direction from Salt Lake, hidden records are concealed. This gorge is newly made, geologically.

And it shall come to pass that the climate will not follow its proper seasons, and the leaves shall fall from the trees in the spring. I see a mighty hail storm coming, and it shall come upon the ungodly and destroy the crops of the earth. A frozen hail stone is shown to me of enormous size, it being several feet thick.

And in that time, rain shall beat against houses with fierce and sweeping winds. Thunder will roar continually, and lightning shall flash with blinding streaks. Quick moving clouds shall appear, and giant hail stones raining down from the sky shall pierce big holes through buildings and automobiles; and the hearts of men shall be filled with fear.

People's bodies are now charged with downward flows of electricity instead of upward flows. The downward flows have a destructive influence upon their bodies, while the upward flows have a good influence. For this reason shall great distress be caused among the people.

I see carrots brought in out of the field freshly dug, yet they are wilted and become soft, having lost their freshness and good flavor, because of the wrong charge of electricity.

The sun shall be seen to fail to follow its true course, and the earth shall be thrown out of its regular way, and the hills shall crumble down and rocks shall fall from their places, and the whole earth shall tremble and shake. I see the sun, and it is sinking low in the northeast, and I see two kinds of clouds, those that are split up by conflicting currents of air, and those that travel with the wind. I see bright sunshine and then dust comes in whirlwinds over the ground. Then darkness suddenly comes and I see the stars, and some appear like they are falling. Thus a great darkness shall come in the daytime, and it shall cause great confusion to many. Cities will be without light, and so great shall be the darkness that many caught away from home shall not be able to find their way back.

Water shall spring forth out of the ground with much pressure, and shall rush down over cliffs and down canyons in increasing volume until it floods the lower lands. And the ground shall cave in with deep and wide cavings, and water shall rush into them; and fire and smoke shall be seen.

I am shown, and I look up into the sky and see another planet slightly towards the north or in a northerly direction; and I see that it is similar to our own earth. I see that it is a land of green vegetation, and streams, and creeks of water like unto our own planet. As I look upon it, I see that it is close enough to our earth that its clouds and the clouds of our earth come together and mix and pass by one another. I see a dark strange cloud with whitish smaller clouds around it, and it comes down low over the hills leaving a white snow covered strip of country underneath it and behind it.

And now after this time, I see a lowland country in the region of the North Pole, and it is overshadowed and surrounded by mountains of ice, excepting one outlet where the ice is melted away. I see that this land is warm, that it is cultivated and its vegetation is abundant, and that it is inhabited by many of the Lost Tribes.

I see the last of many dwellings finished in Salt Lake Valley, and I see the water rising up until the buildings are submerged and the people are forced to leave. I even see the great Temple of the Lord half under water, and the water still rising. Later on, the water subsides, and the valley is reoccupied.

After the time of desolation, the same land that was desolate shall now become rich in vegetation, and I see the whole land luxuriant with vegetation, trees and undergrowth, which before was desert wasteland.

I see Salt Lake in the near future with her habitation numbered by the mile, or miles, instead of blocks. I also see around about a new beautiful country of choice vegetation, especially of fruits and food stuffs, growing rank, large and rich, with no noxious weeds.

I suddenly see the Lord Jesus Christ come in a cloud out of the Eastern Heaven with great brightness. I am taken up suddenly from those around me to meet Him, not even having time to tell them that the Lord is coming to redeem the earth. I see that He has come surprisingly quick, and that this time is shortly before us. I see that He is wearing about a four-inch red stripe over His shoulder and down across His breast, and that the rest of His robe is very white. I see that His coming is very soon, and that because of the suddenness of His coming, many of us will not have the time to properly dress ourselves to meet Him. Thus is the glorious coming of Christ to rule and reign on the earth for a thousand years as King of Kings, Lord of Lords.

I see immortal people walking forth from low clouds. I shake hands with them and recognize them as of many nationalities. I see many resurrected women, some with babies in their arms who were taken from them by death, but now are theirs again to raise to maturity.

The Indians or Lamanites shall become a white and delightsome people. They will move north into Canada where they will have more range for their cattle. I see three generations; a grandmother who is quite dark, a mother who is not quite so dark, and a daughter who is white.

A new and different kind of airship shall come that shall have no wings and no gasoline motors, nor carry fuel of any kind; its shape being something like a ball which carries within itself the necessary electrical instruments which control the power of gravity over it so that the ship may be maneuvered through the air at a snail's pace or very swiftly as preferred. And I see many finer ships come after it with many new improvements, but of the same flying principles. These are heavier than air machines and very commonplace.

God has given some men double the brains of others, to develop and increase in knowledge. To some He has given seven-fold, with sufficient periods of time for development; and unto others He has given more, and unto others less. And this He has given unto them before they were born into the world.

I see ancient men compared with our present-day men, and the ancient man is far superior to our present-day man in faith, in truth, and in the ways of God.

I see an old gray headed man who has the mind of a 16-year-old; he has patterned his life after his own ignorant desires. I also see another man who is around 90 years old, or a hundred, who is not gray, but looks young. He has kept the commandments of God and obeyed the word of wisdom in all things.

And now I, Alma, do declare unto you my brothers and sisters, that these things are all true, and shall shortly come to pass according to the Word of God, for they are made known unto me through the Holy Ghost, which does bear witness of the Father and the Son. And now, do not thank me for these things, but thank God, your Father in Heaven. Even so, Amen.

Moses Thatcher

"Would to God we had statesmen with eyes clear enough to see!.... the day is not far distant, unless the Democratic and Republican parties open their eyes to the situation, when desolation and war will be in this government.

I will say when this nation, having sown to the wind, reaps the whirlwind; when brother takes up sword against brother; when father contends against son, and son against father; *when he who will not take up his sword against his neighbor must needs flee to Zion for safety—then I would say to my friends come to Utah; for the judgments of God, commencing at the house of the Lord, will have passed away, and Utah, undisturbed, will be the most delightful place in all the Union. When war and desolation and bloodshed, and the ripping up of society come upon the nation, I have said to such, "Come to Utah and we will divide our morsel of food with you, we will divide our clothing with you, and we will offer you protection."*

I will tell you, my brethren and sisters, the day will come, and it is not far distant, when he who will not take up his sword against his neighbor, will have to flee to Zion for safety; and it is presupposed in this prediction that Zion will have power to give them protection. We are not going to do it outside of the government, either; we are going to do it inside the government. There is no power in this land to turn this people against the government of the United States. They will maintain the Constitution of this country inviolate, and although it may have been torn to shreds they will tie it together again, and maintain every principle of it, holding it up to the downtrodden of every nation, kindred, tongue and people, and they will do it, too, under the Stars and Stripes. They will stand with their feet firmly upon the backbone of the American continent and maintain the principles which cost their fathers so much, and those principles cannot be taken away by men who violate their oath of office, and betray their trust.

I tell you that there are boys growing up in these mountains who have the principles of human liberty grounded deep in their hearts, and they will maintain them, not only for themselves, but for others. God speed the day I say—if the nation pursues its downward course and tears up these fundamental principles of government which have made them strong—when the Constitution may be rescued and all men and women shall be free again." – Elder Moses Thatcher JOD 26:36

The Cardston Temple, Canada Vision by Sols Caurdisto - 1921

We have been to the Temple erected by your church wherein are to be performed the sacred rites in accordance with your faith. The first time I was strongly impelled to describe to you my impressions. I did so but before the completion of the letter, I received some news that so affected me that acting upon the spur of the moment, I destroyed the document in its entirety.

The continued feeling within me of dissatisfaction as to something left undone, coupled with the desire upon the part of the members of my household who had not visited the temple, led to our second visit to Cardston, in which you so kindly consented to accompany us, notwithstanding the inclement weather and personal inconvenience to yourself which the journey entailed.

It was because of this and many other evidences of your friendship that has given me the privilege to presume to bother you with what after all may be foolish fantacies of a too impressionable mentality. To me it does seem so, for never before in my life have such powerful impressions been infringed upon my inner consciousness as during my visit thru the Temple. Especially was this true at our second visit. The impressions of our first visit were repeated with such overwhelming intensity and variety of detail that I must positively inform you of my experience.

It seems to me it were a sacred duty upon my part to do this, and knowing as I do that your friends will lightly ridicule what to me is a personal matter, I am going to give you in detail my experience in the hope, that if it is well, maybe it is something more than imagination, that you and others of your faith may wisely analyze and correctly use whatever may be gleaned from this letter.

A fortress in time of storm, was the first thought that shaped itself in my mind with my first view of this ancient, yet modern temple; mellowed with the spiritual usage of ancient civilization and customs, yet alert, virile, and watchful.

A grand, solemn, strong, beautiful, useful house of spiritual progression which seemed to be the embodiment of architectural expression of ancient civilization and glories suddenly re-incarnated and for a future and higher civilization than our own. Strength and beauty exaggerated the more flimsy houses and buildings of the town and gave a painfully obvious example of how the soul within is expressed thru the material body, either in the individual or nation, or a race, either in the man or his architecture. Try how I would I could not get away from the feeling that the town itself was inferior to the latest building, so new and yet so old. Even the electric lights failed to change this thought, that the Temple and the town represented two different epochs of humanity's spiritual development expressed in architecture. The town embodied the present epoch, science, art, invention harnessed purely for trade or commerce, irrespective of past or future development. The Temple embodies the accumulated knowledge of the ancient world combined with the modern inventions of science and inspiration as the road to a higher future development so near at hand. Let me put it down even another way.

There is a place called Cardston. A Temple linking the past with the present has been built at Cardston and the town has become a collection of flimsy huts nestling at the foot of the Temple which will continue to function for the spiritual purposes for which it is raised.

Just as the exterior impressions compared with the present and future epochs so did the interior also reflect comparison. Of the beautiful and artistic effects I need not dwell; abler pens can describe the interior from this viewpoint. Sufficient for me to say that the shape of the Temple is a cross, that each apartment is symbolical in artistic and structural effects of some stage of humanity's progress thru the ages. In fact, everything physical is a stepping stone to spiritual progress as such is typified in these ceremonies.

All this was kindly and intelligently explained to us by Mr. Duce on one occasion and by Mr. Wood on the second visit; but I am afraid I was very indifferent and inattentive upon both occasions, for which I tender them my sincere apologies. I had no intentions of being rude or discourteous, but from the moment of entering the Temple until leaving, I was placed in the position of having, as it were, to listen to and grasp a dual narrative all the time, with the result that so engrossed was I at times that I am afraid I was so absent-minded as to appear inattentive if not positively stupid.

I have stated that my impression of the exterior of the building was that of a place of waiting for a higher civilization than our present one. This would suggest a condition of emptiness, but that is not what I mean. An ordinary newly erected building has no atmosphere at all until it has been inhabited some time; after which, it has, as it were, a living atmosphere. What kind of an atmosphere this is, is largely determined by the spiritual development and thought of the persons using and inhabiting the building. This applies especially to places of worship or consecration, and is very noticeable to a sensitive person. Sometimes such an atmosphere is agreeable, exalting, etc.; sometimes very much the reverse, depending upon the spiritual harmony or otherwise of the persons under this atmospheric rule; but was not so as far as it was concerned while outside the Temple.

I could not understand the overwhelming scene of ancient atmosphere which the building actually possessed in its very granite blocks in spite of the fact that I know a few months previous these stones had been laid, yet the feeling of age predominated. I dismissed the feeling as well as I could by thinking that the place of the structure was responsible for the suggestion of age, but when I entered the Temple, how quickly I found there was nothing to suggest to me that present atmosphere of which I have spoken, but was it empty? Emphatically no! Time and again as I listened to the speaker explaining some phase of the building or its meaning, I would be seeing beyond him some illustration of kaleidoscopic nature, depicting what he was describing, only more completely and vividly. The characters were so plain to me that I required all my self control to keep silent from room to room. This continued and only ceased when we were out in the frost and snow once more.

There was no set plan for presenting these pictures to me. It seemed as if when I thought something mental, a picture instantly presented itself in explanation of some word of the conductor, which would have the same effect. I was not afraid, only awed by the wonder of it all and the fearful impressive feeling that I received which seemed to imbed every little detailed scene into my brain, from which it will ever remember and record; and vivid as all of it was, these incidents herein related are the ones upon which I received instructions.

The scenes which I observed of an historical character seemed chiefly to verify and amplify the speaker's outline of past history, and so I do not feel impressed to record such, except to state that the same patriarchal characters whom I observed directing and influencing the early movements of the Church, were the same down through every age and epoch, and as the scenes advanced to more modern times, I saw among these spiritual characters and counselors, persons whose features I had previously observed as being in the material body on other historical occasions.

It seemed as though the temple was filled with the actual spiritual bodies of these previous leaders of your church, each seeming to have the work that person was engaged in whilst in the flesh. In that temple I saw persons who were leaders of your church, during its march across the American desert now engaged in helping these higher patriarchs under whose orders they seemed to be working. It was these latter spiritual leaders, if I may use that term, who seemed to be instructed to show me the scenes here recorded.

I can give no time as to the happening, except that the impressions I received were of actual present or immediate future. I saw first a brief but comprehensive sketch of the present state of the world, or as you would term it, the Gentile Kingdoms. Each country in turn was shown, its anarchy, hunger, ambitions, distrusts and warlike activities, etc., and in my mind was formed from some source the words, "As it is today with the Gentiles."

I saw international war again break out with its center upon the Pacific Ocean, but sweeping and encircling the whole globe. I saw that the opposing forces were roughly divided by so-called Christianity on the one side, and by the so-called followers of Mohammed and Buddha on the other. I saw that the great driving power within these so-called Christian nations, was the Great Apostasy of Rome, in all its political, social and religious aspects. I saw the worldwide dislocation and devastation of production and slaughter of people occur more swiftly and upon a larger scale than ever before. I saw an antagonism begin to express itself from those so-called Christian nations against your people. I saw those with a similar faith to yours in the far east begin to look toward Palestine for safety.

I saw the international world war automatically break down, and national revolution occur in every country, and complete the work of chaos and desolation. I saw geological disturbances occur, which helped in this work as if it were intended to do so. I saw the Cardston Temple preserved from all of this geological upheaval. I saw the international boundary line disappear as these two governments broke up and dissolved into chaos. I saw race rioting upon the American continent on a vast scale.

I saw hunger and starvation in this world; I saw disease produced by hunger, strife and chaos complete the end of this present order or epoch. How long these events were in reaching this consummation I do not know, but my impression was from the outbreak of the international war these things developed into a continuous procession, and almost ran concurrently, as it is with a sickness, the various symptoms are all in evidence at one and the same time, but in different stages of development.

My intensified thought was "What of the Church," if such is to become of the Kingdoms of the earth? Was immediately answered by a subconscious statement. "As it is in the church today," and I saw these higher spiritual beings throughout the length and breadth of the air, marshalling their spiritual forces, and concentrating them upon the high officials of your church upon earth.

I saw the spiritual forces working upon those officers, impressing and moving them, influencing and warning them. I saw the spiritual forces begin to unfold these things into the minds of your elders and other high officials, especially during their spiritual devotions and official duties, and those activities which exalt the mind of the individual or groups. I saw the impressions take hold and inspire the more receptive and spiritual men, until it was all clearly revealed to them in the way the spiritual patriarch desired.

Again I seemed to hear the words, "As it will be." I saw the high officials in council, and under inspired guidance issue instructions to your people to re-consecrate their lives and energies to their faith, to voluntarily discipline themselves, by abstaining from all those forms of indulgence which weaken the body, sap the mentality and deaden the spirit, or waste the income.

I saw further on, instructions given whereby places of refuge were prepared quietly but efficiently by inspired elders. I saw Cardston and the surrounding foothills, especially north and west, for miles, being prepared as a refuge for your people quietly but quickly.

I saw elders still under divine guidance, counseling and encouraging the planting of every available acre of soil in this district, so that large supplies would be near the refuge. I saw the church property under cultivation of an intensified character, not for sale or profit, but for the use of the people. I saw artesian wells and other wells dug all over that territory so that when the open waters were polluted and poisoned that the people of the church and their cattle should be provided for.

I saw the fuel resources of the district develop in many places and vast piles of coal and timber stored for future use and building. I saw the territory carefully surveyed and mapped out, for the camping of a great body of the people of the church. I saw provision also made for a big influx of people who will not at first belong to the church, but who will gather in their tribulation.

I saw vast quantities of surgical appliances, medicines, disinfectants, etc., stored in the temple basement. I saw inspiration given the elders whereby the quantity, quality and kind of things to be stored were judged, which might not be attainable in this territory in time of chaos. I saw defensive preparations working out the organizations of the camps on maps.

I saw the mining corridors used as places of storage underground: I saw the hills surveyed and corrals built in sequestered places for cattle, sheep, etc., quietly and quickly. I saw the plans for the organization of the single men and their duties, the scouts, the guards, the nurses, the cooks, the messengers, the children, the herders, the temple guards, etc.. I saw these things going on practically unknown to the Gentile world, except the Great Apostasy, whose knowledge and hatred is far reaching, in this day of its temporary power. This was going on piece by piece as the Elders were instructed so to do.

I saw the other officials obeying the inspired instructions, carrying their message and exhorting the people to carry out, from time to time the revelation given them, whilst all around throughout the Gentile world the chaos developed in its varying stages, faction against faction, nation against nation, but all in open or secret hostility to your people and their faith. I saw your people draw closer and closer together, as this became more tense and as the spiritual forces warned them through the mouth of your elders and your other officers. I saw the spiritual forces influencing those members who had drifted away, to re-enter the fold. I saw a greater tithing than ever before. I saw vast quantities of necessaries supplied by members whose spiritual eyes had been opened. I saw a liquidation of properties and effects disposed of quietly but quickly by members of the church, as the spiritual influences directed them.

I saw the inspired call sent forth to all the church, to gather to the refuges of Zion. I saw the stream of your people quietly moving in the direction of their refuge. I saw your people moving more quickly and in larger numbers until all the stragglers were housed. I saw the wireless message flashed from Zion's refuge to Zion's refuge in their several places that all was well with them, and then the darkness of chaos closed around the boundaries of your people, and the last days of tribulation had begun.

Sols Caurdisto

The Dream of Plagues

The Dream of the Plagues (1884)

Author unknown. "Vision of Plagues". The Contributor. August 1884, 5:411

The present times seem to be more than usually prolific of prophetic dreams among the Latter-day Saints. In nearly every settlement the people have been warned of events soon to occur; and visions of the future glory of the Kingdom of God upon this earth have passed like a panorama before many of those who love God and obey His commandments.

Some two or three years ago, I had retired for the night, when suddenly a glorious messenger appeared at my bedside and awoke me from my slumber. The light of his presence filled the room, so that objects were discerned as clearly as at noonday.

He handed me a book, saying, "Look, and see what is coming to pass." I took the book in my hands and, sitting up in bed, examined it carefully and read its contents. In size this book was about seven by ten inches, opening like a copybook and bound in beautiful cover, on the front of which was stamped in gold letters its title, which was The Book of the Plagues. The leaves were printed only on the front side of each, and were composed of the very finest quality of pure white linen, instead of paper. The typography throughout was in the finest style of the printer's art. Each page was composed of a picture printed in colors as natural as art can copy nature, which occupied the upper half of the space, below which was the printed description of the scene represented.

On the first page was a picture of a feast in progress, with the long table set upon a beautiful lawn, over which were interspersed clumps of fine shrubs and towering trees. In the background through the foliage, could be discerned a stately suburban villa, adorned with all the ornaments of modern architecture. The landscape presented the appearance of midsummer. The sky, and indeed the whole atmosphere, appeared of a peculiar sickly brassy hue, similar to that which may be observed when the sun is wholly eclipsed, and the disc is just beginning again to give its light. Throughout the atmosphere small white specks were represented, similar to a scattering fall of minute snowflakes in winter. About the table a part of richly dressed ladies and gentlemen were seated in the act of partaking of the rich repast with which the table was laden. The minute specks falling from above were dropping into the food apparently unheeded by all, for a sudden destruction had come upon them. Many were falling backward in the agonies of a fearful death; others drooping upon the table, and others pausing with their hand still holding the untasted food, their countenances betraying a fearful astonishment at the peculiar and unlooked for condition of their companions. Death was in the atmosphere; the judgments of God had come upon them as silently and swiftly as upon the proud Sennacharib and his host of Assyrians.

In one corner of this picture was a small circular vignette, showing the front of the store of a dealer in pork. The wide sidewalk was covered by an awning supported on posts at the outer edge, and on this walk were shown barrels of pork, long strings of sausages, fresh slaughtered hogs, piles of smoked bacon and headcheese; and along the edge of the walk, next to the store, beneath the front windows, leaned a number of large hams and pieces of side meat, reaching across the whole front, except a small space at the doorway. There were twelve of these pieces, and on each piece was painted a large letter, in order to make as a whole the word ABOMINATIONS.

Below this scene was the description: A Feast among the Gentiles, commencement of the Plague. And in smaller type below [was] a note saying that the particles of poison, though represented in the picture, are so small as to be invisible to the naked eye.

On the next page was another picture. It was a street scene in a large city. In the foreground were the residences of wealthy city merchants. The character of the buildings gradually changed; along the view and in the distance were shown the great buildings of trade and commerce in the heart of a large metropolis. On the sidewalks throughout the long vista, the busy, throbbing rushing crowd had been cut down like grass before the mower.

Again it was a midsummer scene. The same atoms of poison were falling through the air, but their work was done; the same sickly brazen atmosphere that seemed thick with foul odors laid upon the earth, in which no breeze stirred a leaf of the foliage. Upon the balconies of the richly decorated residences, across the thresholds of the open doorways, along the walks and upon the crossings, lay the men, women and children, who a few days before were enjoying all the pleasures of life. Further on, the dead were everywhere. Houses of business that had been thronged with customers stood with open doorways, frowning upon streets covered with the dead. Across the thresholds of the banks lay the guardians of wealth, but no thieves were there to take the unlocked treasures within. The costly merchandise of a thousand owners laid untouched upon the counters and shelves. In the noonday glare of the sickly sun, not a soul was shown alive; not one had been left to bury the dead—all had been stricken or had fled from the death-dealing plague and the doomed city. Along midway upon the street, a hungry drove of those horrible ugly slaughterhouse dogs, (which may be seen in the pens attached to the filthy slaughtering places in the outskirts of many cities), was tearing and devouring the dead and feasting upon the bodies of rich and poor alike with none to molest them.

Below this picture was the description: Progress of the Plague among the Gentiles. A street scene in a large city. Nearly fifty of these pictures I carefully observed, wherein the fearful effects of this and other plagues were almost as vividly portrayed as if I had actually seen them.

The last scene in the book was descriptive of the same plague as the first. A beautiful park-like, grassy prairie was surrounded by elm and cottonwood trees, the area embraced being about eighty rods across. In the center of this enclosure was a large cone-shaped tent of a bright purple color, about thirty feet in height by twenty in diameter at the base. Midway in height in this tent was a floor dividing the inside into two stories. Near this tent was another, a round wall tent, about thirty feet in diameter, and nearly as high as the first. This was clean and white. Leaving a space of about a hundred yards from these central tents were hundreds of small rectangular wall tents in rows, reaching as far as the surrounding trees, each tent clean and white, and appearing to be of a size suited to the wants of an ordinary family. Not a human being, animal, bird or vehicle was in sight. Not a breath of air appeared to be stirring. The same atmosphere as in the previous pictures, with the atoms of poison, was represented, and the same time and season of the year.

Below this picture was the description: "A camp of the Saints who have gathered together and are living under the daily revelations of God, and are thus preserved from the plague." I understood from this that each family was in its tent during the hours of the day that the poison falls, and thus were preserved from breathing the deathly particles.

Handing the book to the messenger, who all this time had remained by my side, he vanished from my view as suddenly as he had appeared. I awoke my wife, who was soundly sleeping, and commenced to relate to her what I had just beheld. After telling her the description of the two pictures at the beginning of the book, and commencing on the third, this third picture and all up to the last was suddenly taken from my memory, so that I have never been able to recall them; but still I remember that they were scenes about the plagues and judgments.

THE VISION OF M. SIRRINE England--1846

Dear Brother Hyde, I take the opportunity to drop these few lines to you. I am not in the habit of repeating dreams or visions, but in consequence of the heavenly impression that a certain dream or vision left on my mind, I thought that I would relate it to you.

I preached in Bolton on the evening of the 16th of December (1864), on the resurrection of the dead. After meeting I went to the house of one of the brethren, and retired to bed at about eleven o'clock at night. I had not been in bed long before this singular occurrence took place.

I viewed myself traveling in company with two or three of my brethren in the ministry, and we were conversing on the principles of the kingdom of God, when, all at once, a very fine looking man fell in company with us. He said, "Well, brethren, how do you all do?" We looked at him, and said, "You have got the advantage of us, for we do not know you." He said, "If you will keep it to yourselves whilst I am with you, I will tell you who I am." We told him we would. By this time we had arrived at a brother's house, where we intended to stay all night, for it was then getting evening. We all went in, and were seated in a private room, when the following conversation took place.
[90] Said the stranger to us, "My name is James. I am one of the twelve apostles that was on this earth in the days of our Saviour, and you now see my resurrected body. Handle me, and see; for a spirit hath not flesh and bones as you see me have." We then viewed him very closely, but, oh, the beauty and glory of that body; would to God that I had language to describe it. His flesh and skin looked so beautiful and pure, and his cheeks bloomed like the rose. I then took my hand and laid it on his cheek, but he said to me, "be careful, do not handle me too much, for I am very choice of my immortal body."

Said I, "Brother James, how did the people treat you and the rest of the Saints in that age of the world?"

Said he, "Very much the same as they treat you and the twelve at the present time; they mocked and derided us; our names were cast out as evil; the priests contended with us; they told the people we were false prophets, imposters, and not fit to live on the earth, just as the people say at the present day about the twelve that God has sent in this dispensation."

"The truth is," continued he, "the people are the same now that they were then, and the pure principles of Christ they will not receive, any more at the present day than they would when we told them the truth; and in that day only a few believed our testimony, and but few will receive the truth at the present day."

Said I, "Brother James, the people have got a chapel reared to your name in this country; I wonder if they would let you preach in it."

[91] "Oh no," said he. "They would not let me preach in their chapel any more than they would one of the twelve of the present age; for if I should, my preaching would come in direct opposition to all their false traditions. You know my writings. What little of them they have, they do not practice, although they are not half so plain as when I wrote them, for the plainest part of my writings they have taken away, and if I should go and tell them of it, they would not believe me. So all that can be done is to preach where you can get an opportunity, and gather out the honest; then the rest will be cut off from

the earth, for all the Lord does is to warn people, and when they reject His warning, He cuts them off from the earth by His judgments."

I then said to him, what do you think of P. P. Pratt's poem that he has written to his wife and family at Council Bluffs, Missouri? He replied that it was very good; it expresses the feelings of his heart in a plain and forcible manner. He further added that there once lived a sister in Rome who wrote a piece of poetry on the persecutions that we pass through, which I think full as good as Brother Pratt's; she was a faithful sister, had great faith in the twelve apostles, for I taught her myself the pure principles of the gospel.

I then asked him what he thought of the twelve apostles that we had now with us, that are the leaders of the Church of Jesus Christ, of Latter-day Saints. Said he, "They are good men, and if the Saints will follow their counsel, they will be exalted in the kingdom of God."

Said I, "They have learned many great and glorious principles since the organization of the church."
"Yes," says he, "but they are all but babes yet to what they will be when they get their immortal bodies, as you now see me have."

Said I, "How long have you had your resurrected body?" He did not answer me definitely, but said it had been some time.

Said I to him, "I wish that I had my immortal body, as I see you have; how glad I should be."
Says he, "It will not be long, if you are faithful, before you and all the rest of the Saints will have just such a body as you see me have."

By this time, I thought that supper was ready, and we were called into another room. He said, "If you will not tell who I am, I will take supper with you."

At this I awoke, and behold, it was a dream. Some may think that it was nothing but a phantom of the brain, but to me it was something glorious and tangible, and which I never shall forget in time nor in eternity; for it is verily true, just as I have related it, and it makes my heart rejoice every time I think of it.
Oh, the beauty and glory of that body! Language cannot describe it; therefore, I feel willing to pass through sorrow and affliction whilst in this mortal body, that I may obtain a glorious resurrection. Even so, Amen.

[93] I remain, as ever, your friend and brother in the gospel. M. SIRRINE. (Manchester, December 24, 1846; Millennial Star, Vol. 9:29)

Gayle Smith - (dream was when she was in full standing, currently excommunicated)

I was told it will actually begin in the United States. I know that economies of other countries have been in near collapse, but what I saw was that it starts in the United States. The reason behind the collapse is to bring down America. I don't think they want to totally destroy America. They just want to bring it under their control. Concerning the economic collapse, my mother said I would hear rumors and then they will get louder and then the collapse happens real quickly. I was told just recently that we'll go to bed one night and everything will seem fairly normal. We will wake up the next morning and it will have happened. So it will literally happen overnight or over a weekend like Friday to Monday. When she said you'll hear rumors and then they'll get louder, I've watched that happening and they're getting much louder right now. I was also told that before the crash takes place my mother-in-law would pass away shortly before all these things began. She passed away the 7th of October 1998, The question is, how long is shortly?

I was also told about President Clinton. I was told that Clinton is not really the one they want. They want Gore in there but they think that Gore isn't electable. I was also told that they would either impeach or assassinate Clinton. It would be his choice depending on if he would step down or whether he refuses.

After the economy collapses I saw marauding bands or gangs running around. People just go crazy and they start rioting, looting and killing because they're angry. Everything they know of value on this earth is being taken away from them within a few short days. We've had so much in this country, more than any other country in the world. They're angry at first and then they go crazy because they're hungry. In a very short period of time there will be a famine like we've never seen before. I believe for the most part this famine is brought upon us. It's premeditated and planned out. No one works. No trucks bring food deliveries. Famine is brought on very quickly as stores are cleaned out within hours. There is nothing to eat so people kill others because they are hungry. After a time they begin to kill because they enjoy it. All of them become very depraved. I saw these marauding bands doing awful sadistic sexual acts, cannibalism, eating people while they are still alive and kicking. I always wonder how the Lord would determine who the righteous and who the wicked were. There is a little bit of bad in the best of us and a little bit of good in the worst of us. He doesn't decide that, we do that by our choices depending on how we react to these things that are happening to us. For example, if we saw some of these military people or marauding bands torturing or killing family members I was told that I can have no anger, hatred, bitterness or revenge in my heart for what these people are doing or I would take the first step of being like they are. Our choices determine which side we will stand on. I saw a huge gulf between the righteous and the wicked. You are either depraved and extremely wicked and act like beasts or you will stand on the righteous side with the Lord and you will become increasingly more righteous and in tune with our Father in Heaven.

A short period of time after the economic collapse we are put under the control of FEMA and martial law. The first' thing they do is to close down all the roads and accesses out of the cities. Next they cut communications and conduct house to house searches for food, guns and ammunition. I saw them taking warm boots and warm clothing because it was getting cold and winter was coming. The martial law is so oppressive. It is very similar to what the Nazis did to the Jews. I saw them relocating and sorting families, men from the women, women from the children. I saw two lines. Those too old or young or too feeble to work go to the concentration execution camps while the others are sent to work camps. They put us under a night time curfew and anyone caught out after dark is immediately shot and killed. It is illegal to pray, attend church and hold meetings. I saw an underground resistance set up trying to help get people out of the city to safety. If you don't take the mark, you will be on the run continually. Travel from city to city, county to county or state to state will be hindered unless you have the proper papers to do so.

I saw that the soldiers came to my house and broke the door down. They had orders to take me to be executed. 1 didn't know what to do because there were about six soldiers and just me. I said to the Lord. "If it be Thy will and I'm not to die at this point save me by showing me what to do." I was told to tell them not to touch me or you'll die. I did and the soldiers laughed at me. One of them came up to me and grabbed me by the arm and he immediately dropped dead at my feet. That scared them and they backed out down the stairs. I heard them building up their courage saying things like he must have had a heart attack or something. So they came back to me again and another one came up to me. I told him too that if he touched me he would die. He reached out and grabbed my arm and dropped dead at my feet. This time the rest of the soldiers were terrified. They gathered up their dead friends and didn't touch anything that was mine and left. I was told that if the Lord was willing to exert this much power to protect one person imagine what He would do to protect a group of people gathered in His name. I was told that this is what truly Zion is. It's not necessarily a place but rather it's the people that are the pure in heart who are gathered in His name.

The next scenario I saw was that the animals turn on people. The Hopi Indians have also suggested this will happen. I saw wild animals coming into the cities just devouring people. I saw mountain lions grouping together, Even though they are solitary predators and timid of humans, coming into the city attacking and killing people. A group of these came up to me and I was thinking that I was a goner this time. I thought that it worked before so I went to the Lord and said, "if it be Thy will and I'm not to die at this point please save me and show me what do." He said to me to just reach out and touch the lead lion on the head. I thought, "Oh sure I will." But I did it. As soon as I did it he became as a tame house cat and then all of the other mountain lions did the same. They rubbed up against my leg and rolled over on their backs. Others seeing this were afraid of me. I was told this is like in the scriptures where it says they were afraid to go up against Zion because they are a terrible people. God is with them. These are some of the things they are going to be seeing.

The next scenario I was shown was during the first earthquake in a building with some friends. I knew the building wasn't safe with the earthquake. I opened the door, looked outside and saw the trees failing like dominos all over. I thought how are we going to get out of this. I did the same thing again. I prayed to the Lord, "If it be Thy will and I'm not to die at this time, please save me and tell me what to do." He said to just walk out through the trees. So we walked out through the trees and we were not hurt.

He repeated this over four times to me in different scenarios so it would come automatically to me to go to the Lord. The fourth scenario was that having to be confined to a shelter for two weeks underground. This same one was shown to me 3 times. Anytime it's repeated three times it's very important and you need to pay attention. I thought it had to do with nuclear war or something. At the end of those two weeks I went out because I wanted to see how much damage was done. I went out and walked down the street past this five story building that took up the whole block. As I walked to the center of this block next to the building, the walls of the building started to fall. I looked up and thought what am I going to do now. I'd had enough practice of what to do so I immediately went to the Lord and said, "if it be Thy will and I'm not suppose to die, to please save me and show me what to do." He told me to stoop down right where I was, so I did. As the wall started to fall, I noticed one of the upper windows and the glass had fallen out as it started to fall on me. As it fell, the open frame where the window had fallen out fell around me and I didn't even have a scratch on me. So I was shown that we would be preserved in these miraculous ways and all we have to do is believe and trust in JESUS CHRIST. I was told that our faith will grow with these experiences. As time goes on we'll get faster at knowing what to do. Once we start reacting in the right way and that it works and we're preserved and the Lord is there for us, then our trust and faith builds and we get stronger and more pure. The easy job will be dying. The harder task will be to live through all of these things. Just imagine living through these things and being there when the Lord comes in His glorious second coming. It's all going to be worth it.

Everyone that has food storage will have their life threatened and be forced to turn it in. I was told that the LDS church would call in the food storage, but that they turn it over to the U.N. forces (Note: During Martial Law the church will not fight the troops, nor go against a mandate.). I know that this may be upsetting to some people, but this was repeated to me several times. I was also told that it is very important that I warn people of this! In fact, when I first received this, I cried for three days. I actually had three separate experiences over several days in each of which I was told about the LDS Church calling in food storage and turning it over to the government. If you turn your food in, then you will have to take an identification mark or ID, which is a computer chip implanted in the forehead or the hand. I was shown that when you go in to take the mark, you will have to deny Christ. If you deny Him, you will be given the chip and your life will be preserved. If you refuse, you will be beheaded. I saw many public beheadings. I saw them rounding up patriots and other dissidents and beheading them in public. I thought this was strange that they would use an outmoded way to take life when there were more convenient ways. I was told it was to instill fear.

I saw at the time of the famine that this is when they instigate the mark of the beast. The mark of the beast is a computer chip. It's placed in the hand or in the forehead. I have had someone bring a paper to me about this chip and the technology is in place. It is similar to the ones placed in pets. The chip has in it enough memory to have all your personal information, satellite tracking ability, and a pleasure mode which when implanted gives the host feelings of pleasure so that you are reluctant to give it up. This chip is of organic nature and the body takes it in and nourishes it. I was shown something else about the mark. There's an 18 digit number in the chip which is interesting because 6 + 6 + 6 equals 18. The first three numbers of the chip are 666, which represent the world government. The next 3 numbers are the location or country. USA's number is 1 1 0. The next three digits are your telephone area code. The final nine numbers are your social security number. I was told you wouldn't be able to get a job without the chip. With this technology they will take us into a cashless society where all of your financial activities are known and kept. This mark is an eternal thing. If you take the mark knowingly to preserve your life on this earth, you will forever be aligned with Satan through the eternities and your name is blotted out of the Lamb's Book of Life. When you go to take the mark you will be questioned as to where your loyalties lie. If you don't deny the Savior you are then sent out to be beheaded.

Within 10 days of the economic collapse we have the first earthquake affecting Utah which takes place early in the morning, about 4 or 5 am. When I first saw it I didn't think it was very hard because I saw there wasn't much damage done to my home in Utah County, but it lasts a long time. People will think this is the big one. I saw that this earthquake was much stronger somewhere else like on the west coast area of California but it also affects Nevada. There is a lot of damage done and there is some loss of life though there are a lot of people who survive. The second time my mother showed it to me I realized that it is a very significant earthquake.

The second earthquake affecting Utah takes place about 15 days after the first and also takes place in the early morning around 4 or 5 am. This earthquake is like the world has never seen and affects a much larger area than just Utah. It's right off the Richter Scale. I saw the dams in the mountains in the Wasatch Front area breaking. I don't know if all of them break or if some of them break in the third earthquake, but I know that all of the dams eventually break. I do know that Jordanelle Dam breaks first and comes down and breaks Deercreek Dam. I saw a wall of water 80 feet high come roaring down Provo Canyon with such force it hits houses and they literally explode. When it hits Utah Lake it surges down the Jordan River and it wipes everything out on both sides of the river all the way to the Great Salt Lake. I saw homes out in the west like in Magna and Plains City sinking into the ground like quicksand due to liquefaction. I saw buildings and trees falling like dominos. I saw myself in my home trying to get out the door to safety. I was thrown to the floor with such force that I looked up at the wall and I thought if that wall were to fall on me it would just have to fall because I can't even raise my head up or get to my hands and knees to crawl out of the way to safety. I saw cracks opening up in the earth running from east to west and I thought that was really strange because I thought the faults ran north to south. These cracks open at the Point of the Mountain where the freeway goes over the mountain from Utah County to Salt Lake County, Beck Street in Salt Lake City and at Willard Bay. I saw these huge cracks 600 to 1000 feet deep and 500 to 600 feet across with homes, people and everything falling down into these cracks. They run from the mountain clear out to the valley floors. These cracks separate Utah County from Salt Lake County, Salt Lake County from Davis County, and Davis County from Weber County. I think these cracks may open in the 2nd or 3rd earthquakes but I really don't know. I know that later I saw molten lava coming up through these cracks in the earth. I saw a huge volcano in Northern California, one in Southern Idaho and one in the Yellowstone caldera. I think that the volcanoes start with the 3rd earthquake because I saw that it was daytime and the 3rd and 4th earthquakes happen in the afternoon. I saw volcanoes right here in this Valley and saw hot lava falling on people. I was running from house to house trying to warn them to get out because the volcano was here and ready to blow but they ignored me and were laughing. I finally had to leave because they wouldn't listen. I had a geologist call me after I had been on the radio. He said he had heard what I had said about the earthquakes. He said it was just fascinating to him how I was describing them especially if one doesn't have any knowledge in this area. About the cracks that run east to west, it isn't a fault but fissures that come out from the fault line. Concerning the liquefaction and the things falling like dominos, this is very much like the Mexican earthquake where it's the bottom of a lake with a sandy base and would cause liquefaction. The waves will go out and hit the mountains and bounce back and that's what causes the earthquake to last so long. That's also why it causes the trees and buildings to fall like dominos, one on top of each other. Another thing he said was that the plates underneath the Wasatch Front sit ajar. What he said will happen when we have a big earthquake is that one will raise up and one will drop. That was the force I felt when I was thrown and pinned to the floor.

My mother took me to the Point of the Mountain and I looked as far west, north and south as I could see and both Utah and Salt Lake Valleys were full of water. She brought me over and sat me down right across the street from my house in Lehi and water was lapping right up against my feet. A friend brought a map of the old Lake Bonneville and an elevation map of the area I live in. We found that my home sits at about the 4800 foot level so we figured that's how high the water comes up. I believe this also takes place after the 3rd earthquake and its purpose is to cleanse these valleys of the rest of the wicked.

I also saw an invasion of this country. I saw millions of Chinese coming in along the west coast and down towards the Mexican border. I also saw Russians invading the east coast at the same time. Additionally I saw an army coming down from the north but they didn't get close enough for me to see who they were. I saw thousands of parachutes until they just darkened the sky. I saw individuals coming down on ropes out of helicopters all over. I saw in the beginning of this invasion that there are nuclear explosions on both coasts. I also saw a nuclear explosion north toward Salt Lake City, which could be Hill Air Force Base, but I really don't know for sure. When I was shown these things I went to the Lord and asked how we could possibly survive all this. I saw that this invasion takes place on a holiday when families get together and eat which I believe could be either Thanksgiving or Christmas but it could be New Years.

There were also diseases so terrible like the Ebola Virus. I saw people bleeding from the eyes, nose, ears, mouth and from every orifice of the body and dying very quickly.

Later I saw that the poles of the earth reverse. Before the pole shift it is very still and quiet. Then I saw such horrendous winds that caused boulders the size of houses to fly through the air as the shift takes place. Anything or anyone above ground will not survive because of the winds. There's nothing left standing over two feet above the ground. I also saw a comet that hits the earth. I don't know where the comet or the pole shifts fits into the scenario. I assume they are later because I was shown these things happen after the economic collapse and the earthquakes.

I saw the comet hitting the earth but pieces of it coming and hitting the earth before the main part of the comet. That is what the mighty hailstorm is which is talked about in the scriptures. This fiery hail or the hailstorm that destroys all the crops of the earth according to D & C 29 is actually pieces of a comet coming in from the outer regions. I saw this comet hit in the west. Some people I've talked to say they've seen it hitting in Nevada and others saw it hit in the Pacific Ocean. I never saw where it hit. All I saw was a flash of white light which lights up the whole sky and then it turns blood red starting from the west going to the east. This is what I believe triggers the 4th earthquake that's heard around the world. That's the earthquake I believe when Christ returns.

There's a space between the 3rd and 4th earthquakes in Utah and I don't know how long of a space there is. The 3rd earthquake which takes place in the spring, maybe April, triggers all of these natural calamities that will begin happening all around the earth and the whole earth will be in turmoil; tidal waves 500 feet high, horrendous tornadoes and winds, earthquakes and volcanoes all going on. I was told that only those that are ordained to do so would live through this. So it will not only be the wicked that will be taken off the earth, there will be righteous among them too. If you survive it you will know without a shadow of a doubt that the only way you were able to walk through it is through the power of God.

This is not a message of fear. That's not what I'm about. I'm telling people it will be worth what we have to go through. Everybody asks why get food storage? Why try and prepare? How do we prepare? All I can say is the food storage is necessary, so prepare. I have seen these things and I know they are going to happen. I saw whole subdivisions of homes all totally destroyed except one right in the middle that doesn't even have a broken window. I saw the gas mains breaking and homes exploding one by one up the street and there would be a couple that wouldn't even be touched. To say it will be unusual is an understatement of how things are going to happen because the Lord will preserve those who are ordained to do so. It will be like everyone dying from these horrible diseases and some won't even get them. I saw ways we would be protected which would be nothing less than miraculous. The only way we are going to make it is to have a personal relationship with Jesus Christ. I can't stress hard enough that it is of the utmost necessity to have a personal relationship with and a testimony of Jesus Christ. The testimony of Jesus is the spirit of revelation. Personal revelation is going to be absolutely vital. If you don't have the money to get physically prepared, fine, get prepared spiritually. It's the most important way to prepare. It's only through Jesus Christ that we are going to be saved. These things we will walk through are going to be scary, but it's the only way we can be sufficiently humbled and purified to meet our Savior when he returns. That is what it is really all about.

Before the 3rd earthquake we will be led out by beings of light to cities of refuge or cities of light where we will remain while the rest of the calamities go out to the rest of the world. If you do not make it to one of these cities you will not survive. I SAW THAT ALL THOSE THAT ARE WILLING TO BELIEVE IN JESUS CHRIST AND HAVE FAITH IN HIM AND WILL ACCEPT HIM WILL BE LED OUT. The 3rd earthquake is the removal of the wicked that remain who refuse to accept Jesus Christ. I asked how long we would have to prepare before we are led out. I was told to read Mosiah 24 in the Book of Mormon. I started reading and it was talking about when Alma was under the persecution of the Lamanites. They prayed day and night for relief. The Lord told them to prepare because they were going to be led out the next morning. The Lord shut the eyes of the Lamanites so that they couldn't see and then led them out. That's how I was told it would be. We would have overnight to prepare. I was also told that they would no longer speak about when the children of Israel were led out of Egypt but that the miracles will be so great in these days ahead that they would talk about when we were led out to the New Jerusalem. Whatever we pass through will be a very short period of time and it will be well worth the reward.

The most important reason why I have done this is so I can bear witness of Jesus Christ. Because if we don't have a testimony of Jesus Christ and we don't bear witness of Him, we won't survive. If we are not willing to lay down our lives for our Savior as He laid down His life for us, we just simply won't survive. I know that He lives and I know that He is my Savior and I know that He is in charge. If we aren't willing to give up everything, including our lives, we aren't worthy of Him. The most important thing I can say is to get a personal relationship with Him and get personal revelation because it will be vital and it is the most important thing you can do.

"George Washington's Vision"

This afternoon, as I was sitting at this table engaged in preparing a dispatch, something seemed to disturb me. Looking up, I beheld standing opposite me a singularly beautiful female. So astonished was I, for I had given strict orders not to be disturbed, that it was some moments before I found language to inquire the cause of her presence. A second, a third and even a fourth time did I repeat my question, but received no answer from my mysterious visitor except a slight raising of her eyes.

By this time I felt strange sensations spreading through me. I would have risen but the riveted gaze of the being before me rendered volition impossible. I assayed once more to address her, but my tongue had become useless, as though it had become paralyzed.

A new influence, mysterious, potent, irresistible, took possession of me. All I could do was to gaze steadily, vacantly at my unknown visitor. Gradually the surrounding atmosphere seemed as if it had become filled with sensations, and luminous. Everything about me seemed to rarefy, the mysterious visitor herself becoming more airy and yet more distinct to my sight than before. I now began to feel as one dying, or rather to experience the sensations, which I have sometimes imagined accompany dissolution. I did not think, I did not reason, I did not move; all were alike impossible. I was only conscious of gazing fixedly, vacantly at my companion.

Presently I heard a voice saying, "Son of the Republic, look and learn," while at the same time my visitor extended her arm eastwardly, I now beheld a heavy white vapor at some distance rising fold upon fold. This gradually dissipated, and I looked upon a stranger scene. Before me lay spread out in one vast plain all the countries of the world — Europe, Asia, Africa and America. I saw rolling and tossing between Europe and America the billows of the Atlantic, and between Asia and America lay the Pacific.

"Son of the Republic," said the same mysterious voice as before, "look and learn." At that moment I beheld a dark, shadowy being, like an angel, standing or rather floating in mid-air, between Europe and America. Dipping water out of the ocean in the hollow of each hand, he sprinkled some upon America with his right hand, while with his left hand he cast some on Europe. Immediately a cloud raised from these countries, and joined in mid-ocean. For a while it remained stationary, and then moved slowly westward, until it enveloped America in its murky folds. Sharp flashes of lightning gleamed through it at intervals, and I heard the smothered groans and cries of the American people.

A second time the angel dipped water from the ocean, and sprinkled it out as before. The dark cloud was then drawn back to the ocean, in whose heaving billows in sank from view. A third time I heard the mysterious voice saying, "Son of the Republic, look and learn," I cast my eyes upon America and beheld villages and towns and cities springing up one after another until the whole land from the Atlantic to the Pacific was dotted with them.

Again, I heard the mysterious voice say, "Son of the Republic, the end of the century cometh, look and learn." At this the dark shadowy angel turned his face southward, and from Africa I saw an ill-omened specter approach our land. It flitted slowly over every town and city of the latter. The inhabitants presently set themselves in battle array against each other. As I continued looking I saw a bright angel, on whose brow rested a crown of light, on which was traced the word "Union," bearing the American flag, which he placed between the divided nation, and said, "Remember ye are brethren." Instantly, the inhabitants, casting from them their weapons became friends once more, and united around the National Standard.

"And again I heard the mysterious voice saying "Son of the Republic, look and learn." At this the dark, shadowy angel placed a trumpet to his mouth, and blew three distinct blasts; and taking water from the ocean, he sprinkled it upon Europe, Asia and Africa. Then my eyes beheld a fearful scene: From each of these countries arose thick, black clouds that were soon joined into one. Throughout this mass there gleamed a dark red light by which I saw hordes of armed men, who, moving with the cloud, marched by land and sailed by sea to America. Our country was enveloped in this volume of cloud, and I saw these vast armies devastate the whole county and burn the villages, towns and cities that I beheld springing up. As my ears listened to the thundering of the cannon, clashing of sword, and the shouts and cries of millions in mortal combat, I heard again the mysterious voice saying, "Son of the Republic, look and learn" When the voice had ceased, the dark shadowy angel placed his trumpet once more to his mouth, and blew a long and fearful blast. "Instantly a light as of a thousand suns shone down from above me, and pierced and broke into fragments the dark cloud which enveloped America. At the same moment the angel upon whose head still shone the word Union, and who bore our national flag in one hand and a sword in the other, descended from the heavens attended by legions of white spirits. These immediately joined the inhabitants of America, who I perceived were will nigh overcome, but who immediately taking courage again, closed up their broken ranks and renewed the battle.

Again, amid the fearful noise of the conflict, I heard the mysterious voice saying, "Son of the Republic, look and learn." As the voice ceased, the shadowy angel for the last time dipped water from the ocean and sprinkled it upon America. Instantly the dark cloud rolled back, together with the armies it had brought, leaving the inhabitants of the land victorious!

Then once more I beheld the villages, towns and cities springing up where I had seen them before, while the bright angel, planting the azure standard he had brought in the midst of them, cried with a loud voice: "While the stars remain, and the heavens send down dew upon the earth, so long shall the Union last." And taking from his brow the crown on which blazoned the word "Union," he placed it upon the Standard while the people, kneeling down, said, "Amen."

The scene instantly began to fade and dissolve, and I at last saw nothing but the rising, curling vapor I at first beheld. This also disappearing, I found myself once more gazing upon the mysterious visitor, who, in the same voice I had heard before, said, "Son of the Republic, what you have seen is thus interpreted: Three great perils will come upon the Republic. The most fearful is the third, but in this greatest conflict the whole world united shall not prevail against her. Let every child of the Republic learn to live for his God, his land and the Union." With these words the vision vanished, and I started from my seat and felt that I had seen a vision wherein had been shown to me the birth, progress, and destiny of the United States.

Sampling of Visions Together

References: D&V1 = Dreams & Visions, Volume 1, D&VII = Dreams and Visions Volume II, VG = Visions of Glory. These books also carry quotes from several other books, but I refer you to these sources first for simplicity of finding them.

Economic Collapse

George Albert Smith (p. 36 D&VII) 1930

President at the time will not be of European ancestry. This collapse will make the Great Depression look like a Sunday picnic.

Patriarch Wolfgramm (p. 41 D&VII) 1989

Big financial collapse last two years of a sitting president. There will be a great drought about the same time all over the country. Many in the church will apostatize.

Spencer (VG, p.116) 2011

I saw that whenever this time was that I was being shown, the financial structure of the world had completely collapsed. Every bank had closed down and money was worthless. People are learning to trade and barter. Manufacturing and industry were at a virtual stand-still. There were no raw materials and no money to pay the workers. Factories and global businesses shut down overnight.

Charles Evans (VG, p. 258) 1894

Confidence is lost. Wealth is arrayed against labor, labor against wealth....together with the policy of many wealthy ones, has produced distress and do presage further sorrow. Mad with rage men and women rushed upon each other. Blood flowed down the streets of cities like water.

Sols Caurdisto (VG, p. 251) 1923

I saw the international world war automatically break down, and national revolution occur in every country and complete the work of chaos and desolation. ...I saw the international boundary line disappear (Cananda/US) and these two governments broke up and dissolved into chaos. I saw race rioting upon the American continent on a vast scale.

Sarah Menet, There is No Death

Shopping and buying seemed to stop and the economy failed throughout the world. Few had any money at all, and those who did have it could not buy anything. Gold and silver and other commodities had value and could be traded.

Gayle Smith (personal dream/story on internet) 1993

My mother then started showing me a scenario of events that will take place beginning with a worldwide economic collapse that would take place in the month of October.

I was told it will actually begin in the US. The reason it happens is to bring down America. I don't think they want to destroy America, they just want to bring it under their control. My mother said I would hear rumors and they will get louder and the collapse will happen quickly. We will wake up one morning and it will have happened.

After the collapse I saw marauding bands or gangs running around. People just go crazy and start rioting. They are killing because they are angry and hungry. Everything they know of value on this on this earth is being taken away from them within a few days. In a very short time there will be a famine.

I believe for the most part this famine is brought upon us. It's premeditated and planned out. No trucks bring food deliveries. Famine is brought on quickly and the stores are cleared out within hours. A short term after the collapse we are put under FEMA and Martial law.

Foreign troops are called in America to help restore order, but are here to attack us instead, set off nuclear bombs, usher in New World Order.

George A. Smith (D&VII, p. 35)

*UN troops take away our weapons. *Truck bombs (nuclear) all over the US set off at the same time. *Russia will be the world's military power.

Patriarch Wolfgramm (D&VII, p. 40)

*Nuclear bomb in No. Utah (HAFB)

*Millions of troops invade

Spencer (VG, p.119)

I saw foreign troops landing on the east and west coasts of America. There were tens of thousands of them. They came in large ships, some of them former cruise ships and naval escorts. They landed with thousands of vehicles, most of them laden with relief supplies, but also with large tanks and missile launchers.

In California, some Americans tried to fight the troops because they saw them as invaders.

There were a few battles where the local people lost. The foreign troops did not punish the survivors; they just asked them to cooperate, fed them and released them.

George Washington's Dream (1777)

"...And again I heard the mysterious voice saying, 'Son of the Republic, look and learn.' At this, the dark, shadowy angel placed a trumpet to his mouth and blew three distinct blasts; and taking water from the ocean, he sprinkled it upon Europe, Asia, and Africa. Then my eyes beheld a fearful scene. From each of these countries arose thick, black clouds that were soon joined into one. And throughout this mass, there gleamed a dark red light by which I saw hordes of armed men, who, moving with the cloud, marched by land and sailed by sea to America, which country was enveloped in the volume of cloud. And I dimly saw these vast armies devastate the whole country, and burn the villages, towns and cities that I beheld springing up."

Gayle Smith's Dream

I also saw an invasion of the country. I saw millions of Chinese coming in along the west coast and down towards the Mexican border. I also saw Russians invading the east coast at the same time. Additionally I saw an army coming down from the north, but they didn't get close enough for me to see who they were. I saw thousands of parachutes until they just darkened the sky. I saw individuals coming down on ropes out of the helicopters all over. I saw the beginning of this invasion that there are nuclear explosions on both coasts. I also saw a nuclear explosion north toward SLC which could be Hill Air Force Base but I really don't know for sure. When I was shown these things I went to the Lord and asked how we could possibly survive all this. I saw that this invasion takes place on a holiday when families get together and eat which I believe could be either Thanksgiving or Christmas.

Sarah Menet There is No Death

While viewing the cities of light (tent cities), my focus changed again and I became aware of missiles being launched and hitting US cities. I watch as mushroom clouds started forming over many areas of the states. Some of the clouds came from missiles that I knew were fired from Russia and others were not from missiles at all but from bombs that were already within the US. These latter bombs had been hidden tin trucks and cars and were driven to certain locations and then detonated.

I specifically saw Los Angeles, Las Vegas, and NYC hit with bombs. NYC was hit with a missile, but I think Los Angeles was hit by at least one truck bomb, it not several, because I did not see any missile. I also saw a small mushroom cloud form north of SLC without the aid of a missile.

At almost the same time and in the same locations as the mushroom clouds I saw Russian and Chinese troops invading the US. The Russians were parachuting into many spots along the eastern coast. I also saw them parachuting in Utah. Chinese troops were invading from the west coast near LA. The Chinese and Russians were met with resistance from those who had survived the disease and bombs. I did not see any US military there at that time. I did not see much of this war, but was impressed that it was short in duration and that the troops lost and left.

Earthquake in Utah

Spencer (VG, p. 117)

My flight across North America began in Salt Lake City. There had been a massive earthquake in that area in the fall of the year. The fault that runs along the Wasatch front had moved dramatically, causing a great deal of damage to cities along the front.

I saw that the next spring after the destruction in Utah, there were another devastating series of earthquakes that occurred along the west coast of North and South America. The western coast of CA and Mexico and all the way to the tip of S. America was shaken so badly that much of it broke away from the mainland and formed a series of islands off the coast.

(p 121) Now, back to N. Temple, the earthquake had broken up the streets and where there were cracks in the road, water was shooting into the sky. Water was also gushing from manhole covers, storm drains and cracks in the earth. All this time I was wondering where all the water was coming from. The water was shooting up about six feet into the air. It was all astonishing.

(p. 123) All of this water drained into the Great Salt Lake, moving the salted water in a tidal wave out into the desert northwest of the lake. In some places I-15 was covered and the whole airport was flooded. It was months before military planes could land there.

(p.127) The earthquake had not been centered in downtown SLC but here where the land had dropped away (Draper). Apparently it had been overarching a massive underground lake.

Gayle Smith's Dream (online)

Within 10 days of the economic collapse we have the first earthquake affecting Utah which takes place early in the morning, about 4 or 5 am. When I first saw it I didn't think it was very hard because I saw there wasn't much damage done to my home in Utah County, but it lasts a long time. People will think this is the big one. I saw that this earthquake was much stronger somewhere else like on the west coast area of California but it also affects Nevada. There is a lot of damage done and there is some loss of life though there are a lot of people who survive. The second time my mother showed it to me I realized that it is a very significant earthquake. The second earthquake affecting Utah takes place about 15 days after the first and also takes place in the early morning. This earthquake is like the world has never seen and affects a much larger area than Utah. It's right off the Richter Scale. (All of Utah dams break.)

Kenneth, (D&VII p. 121)

The scene seems to gain some control when, after a little time passed (not sure how long), a second earthquake hit and was worse than the first. Again, more time passed and a third earthquake hit. I thought that not a single building could stand the terrible shaking of the earth. However, looking over the two valleys there were still many buildings standing. Even those that still stood had some degree of damage.

I was able to see the faces of many and the fear of God was definitely there. Not so much fear as in respect, but fear of furthering chastising. Fear was soon replaced by anger and outright defiance of their Maker. How could God-fearing people turn so quickly on their Maker?

Sarah Menet, There is No Death

Now the smoke became very heavy, dark, and thick. Just as things appeared to be as bad as they could get, the earth began to quake. This occurred during a winter, seemingly the winter that followed the very long one I saw earlier. ** (Farmer's Almanac predicts nastiest winter yet for 2013-2014).

The chaos had existed for almost a full year by this time. ** (Contradicts Gayle's "10 days following the collapse.)

The earthquakes began in the West, around Idaho and Wyoming and then quickly spread in every direction. I saw a huge earthquake hit Utah and then California.

(Even with all the earthquakes, the majority of deaths are caused by gangs and marauders. Also, associates the earthquakes with the earth attempting to cleanse itself of the chaos and evil that engulfed the people.)

There are over 50 other dreams I have collected regarding the earthquake to hit SLC. Topics not included here, but addressed: no electricity for years, water scarce and toxic, volcanoes,

A Plague that Kills Approximately 1/3 of the Worlds Population

Spencer (VG, p.128)

About this time, a devastating plague swept across the nation. It came in three waves. Each wave more virulent, killing healthier people, and killing them quicker. It swept across North and South America and around the world killing billions. But the troops who arrived seemed to be mostly immune to it, though a few of them died. It took many months before the survivors of the plague realized the true source of it.

(p.131) About this time, the same plague that had devastated so much of the east arrived in Utah as it spread across the nation. As I said, we found out later that the plague was man-made, and the troops had been inoculated against the pathogen that caused the plague.

(p. 132) When a person contracted the plague, they got many small pox marks on their skin similar to pimples. They grey very sick quickly. The itching and pain were severe. Shortly before death, the pox erupted and oozed. This fluid was extremely contagious. Everyone who touched it got sick. The very young and very old died first. Those who were trying to help others got contaminated by touching the fluid and died next.

...I was left with the impression that between the earthquake and the plague, more than half of the population had been killed--more on the coastlines and fewer inland.

Apostle John Taylor (D&V1 p.35)

This vision is so extensive, I am only going to list the cities he talks of: Salt Lake City, Council Bluffs, Washington DC, Philadelphia, Broadway, NY, Grand Central Park, Missouri, Illinois and Iowa. He reports seeing death on a large scale due to a plague of sickness, violence, murder, fires, no one left to bury the piles of dead people. Major cities evacuated.

Sarah Menet There is No Death

I then saw a man walk into the middle of a crowd of people and drop what seemed like a quart full of liquid. The jar broke and the liquid spread. I understand that people nearby had become infected with a disease from the liquid, and they didn't even know it. A day or two later people became sick and started dying. I saw that this would happen in at least four particular cities: New York, Los Angeles, San Francisco, and Salt Lake City. This disease started with white blisters, some of the size of a dime, appearing on the hands, arms and faces of the victims. The blisters quickly developed into white puffy sores. Those with the disease would stumble around and fall over dead.

I also saw other people with a flu-like virus that spread more quickly than the first disease. The victims had blood coming from their nose, mouth, eyes, and ears. These people died even faster of this disease than the ones who had the first sickness. These diseases became widespread across the US with hundreds of thousands infected. Many died within a short time, perhaps 24 hours.

Charles Evans, (VG, p. 259)

Again the light shone, revealing an atmosphere tinged with a leaden hue which was the precursor of an unparalleled plague whose first symptoms were recognized by a purple spot which appeared on the cheek or on the back of the hand and which invariably enlarged until it spread over the entire surface of the body producing certain death.

The Dream of the Plagues (1884), (VG, p.261)

On the first page was a picture of a feast in progress, with the long table set upon a beautiful lawn, over which were interspersed with clumps of fine shrubs and towering trees. The landscape presented the appearance of midsummer. The sky, and indeed the whole atmosphere appeared of a peculiar sickly brassy hue, similar to that which may be observed when the sun is wholly eclipsed and the disc is just beginning again to give its light. Throughout the atmosphere small white specks were represented, similar to a scattering fall of minute snowflakes in winter.

About the table a party of richly dressed ladies and gentlemen were seated in the act of partaking of the rich repast with which the table was laden. The minute specks falling from above were dropping into the food apparently unheeded by all, for a sudden destruction had come upon them.

(p.264) Below this picture was the description: "A camp of the Saints who have gathered together and are living under the daily revelations of God, and thus preserved from the plague." I understood from this that each family was in its tent during the hours of the day that the poison falls, and thus were preserved from breathing the deadly particles.

The church issues a call out to hide in the mountains for 18-24 months to preserve us from the plague. "Tent Cities" are protected from the troops.

Sarah Menet, There is no Death

As I looked upon this scene of chaos, smoke, and destruction, I noticed there were small pockets of light scattered over the US, perhaps 20 or 30 of them. I noticed that most of the locations of light were in the western part of the US with only three of four of them being in the East. These places of light seemed to shine brightly through the darkness and were such a contrast to the rest of the scene that they caught my full attention. I focused on them for a moment and asked, "What is this light?"

I was then able to see these points of light were people who had gathered together and were kneeling in prayer. The light was actually coming from the people, and I understood that it was showing forth their goodness and love for each other. They had gathered together for safety and contrary to what I had witnessed elsewhere were caring more for each other than for themselves. Some of the groups were small with only a hundred people or so. Other groups consisted of what seemed to be thousands.

I realized that many, if not all, of these places of light, or "cities o flight" had somehow been established just before the biological attack and they were very organized. In these places were relative peace and safety. I noticed the gangs made no threats on these groups. However, the people within had defenses and God was with them.

The Cardston Prophecy (1923) (VG, p.251) (Cardston, Canada Temple)

I saw further on, instructions given whereby places of refuge prepared quietly but efficiently by inspired elders. I saw Cardston and the surrounding foothills, especially north and west for miles, being prepared for your people quietly but quickly. I saw the fuel resources of the district develop in many places and vast piles of coal and timber stored for future use and building. I saw the territory carefully surveyed and mapped out, for the camping of a great body of the people of the church. I saw provisions also made for a big influx of people who will not at first belong to the church , but who will gather in their tribulation. I was these things going on practically unknown to the Gentile world.

I saw the inspired call sent forth to all the church, to gather to the refuges of Zion. I saw the stream of your people quietly moving in the direction of their refuge. I saw your people moving more quickly in larger numbers until all the stragglers were housed. I saw the wireless message flashed from Zion's refuge to Zion's refuge in their several places that all was well with them, and then the darkness of chaos closed around the boundaries of your people, and the last days of tribulation had begun.

BISHOP JOHN H. KOYLE: THE PROPHECIES3

Since he never kept a diary or personal record of any kind, many of the visions and spiritual experiences of Koyle can no longer be accounted for. However, the one experience upon which all sources agree is the vision received in 1894 wherein the mine was revealed to him. On this subject, the following statement was made by Carter E. Grant in a letter to Apostle James E. Talmage on September 30, 1931:

"I heard this story repeated by Brother Koyle in 1911, 1912, 1913, 1914, and 1915, and many times since. One peculiar thing about Brother Koyle, he never crosses himself, repeating his dream with the same exactness as he did in the beginning. One would think he would change it or add to it, but he never has."

The messenger told him the purpose of the mine would be to bring relief to the Lord's faithful people at a time when great tribulation and distress would be in the land. The mine was to be called the "Relief Mine." He told him of a period of four years of famine and explained that the first two years the Saints would be able to get by, but the third and fourth years they would have nothing to eat unless it was prepared and stored up against that time. Then there would be two more years which would be a recovery period. The messenger explained that there would be winters of heavy snow and big snow drifts after which there would be a mild open winter, but whether that winter was to follow immediately or whether some other winters would be in between, he never explained.

However, immediately following the mild open winter, there would be a hot, dry summer. The crops would come up in the spring, and there would be considerable moisture, and the crops would be glorious (that is the word Bishop used to use.) He saw the wheat would grow up and head out beautifully, and the irrigated wheat would mature, but the dry land wheat would not have enough moisture to fill out. By harvest time the heads would curl over in a sort of crescent shape. This was shown to him in another dream wherein he saw he went into the wheat fields when they were binding the grain which looked like it would be a splendid crop. He picked up a bundle of wheat by the binding twine, and the head's end of the bundle came up with the butt end of the bundle hanging down because it was heavier. Realizing that the head end should have gone down if there had been good wheat in it, he examined the heads of wheat by crushing them in his hands to bring out the kernels. He found that the wheat was terribly shrunken and not fit for food. He was told by the messenger that this condition would bring about a shortage of food during the first year of harvest.

The second year he was shown would be the same only much less food raised. Still, the irrigated grain would be good. He was told we would need to store up the first and second years grain to supply food for the third and fourth years. The third year the shortage would be so great that there would hardly be anything raised for food. The fourth year they would not be able to raise anything for food.

He was shown in another dream that during the fourth year there would be plenty of money to buy food and he with others went up and down throughout the country seeking to buy food and they could not buy any. Any people who had a little food would not sell it at any price. During this time of famine there would be no rain to do any good. He saw the clouds would come up, and it would look like it was going to rain, but a wind would come up and blow the clouds away; and if there was any rain at all, it was just a few drops which were not sufficient to do any good.

The purpose of the mine was to build store bins and store up wheat and other foods like Joseph of old who was sold into Egypt. He saw the rains would come in the fifth year, and they would be forced to spare a little wheat for seed but would be sorely pressed to raise enough to eat during the fifth year and save enough for seed for the sixth year. The rains continued to come, the crops grew, and at the harvest time of the sixth year they would have enough food to carry on.

He was told by the messenger that there would be a great crash in the land before the period of famine began. This crash would be brought about by prices going up, which condition was illustrated to him as being like a person on high stilts. When prices became extremely high, something happened in the land like knocking the stilts from under the person and down came everything. Businesses closed down, labor was thrown out of work, people were hungry, and great tribulations were in the land. He saw that the best place to live and to work would be at the mine. Those who worked there would be the best off. He was told by the messenger that the Church program to care for the poor would all be used up during the first and second years of famine, that the mine would bring relief during the third year and would carry on the relief from the third year on.

Koyle gave progress reports of things that would happen inside of the mine and about other things. He gave probably one of these reports each month or so at the Thursday night meetings. This is what kept up a great amount of interest for the miners to look forward to.
Bishop Koyle's Prophecies and revelations are abundant with details of the famines of the last days. Koyle also described this food shortage that had been shown to him in dreams. Grain would grow up as though it would produce a fine crop--but something caused it to shrivel up and become a valueless harvest. Famine would occur all over the world--not only because of crop failures, but because of the troubles and chaos caused by the shutdown of manufacturing and transportation.

At that early date he also said words like these: "By the time we get our ore, the mining districts will be almost at a standstill. These automobiles will get larger and larger, until some of them will resemble street cars, filled with people. Then, too, I saw the farms all though the country all being mortgaged, and as a relief to the condition, the people were coming to borrow money at a low rate of interest from the Koyle Mining Company. I also saw a large bank belonging to our company standing on a certain corner in Spanish Fork. (I have since been shown the corner.) Then I saw the hard times beginning to tell upon the treasury of the Church, being more depleted than in many years. Then, right in the very midst of all these happenings, with things at their darkest, we began shipping ore, giving a decided relief to the situation." ("Grant/Talmage Statement", Sept. 9, 1931, p. 10)

In this section we'll review the many things he foretold to the stockholders.

HORSELESS CARRAGES
The Bishop saw in about 1914 that in time the horses would be left home. The new king of carriages that people would use would have two eyes so they could see at night time. He also saw these new vehicles would get larger and larger until they would become as large as box cars. They would travel through the country at night at a very great speed. Then it would be most unsafe to cross the street day or night.

SPANISH FORK POWER PLANT
About 1910 Koyle told a group that he would buy the dinners for the group if there was not an electric power plant on the Spanish Fork River within a given time. Koyle seemed to always be a winner. In 1911 Koyle told another group he would buy their dinners if there was not a powder plant built on the bench south of Mapleton, Utah. It so turned out that Koyle was right again.

REBUBLICAN ELEPHANT DREAM
Koyle foresaw the Republican victory of 1928 but stated that the man riding the donkey would win in 1932 and continue to win, establishing an unprecedented record of successive victories at the pools. During this time the elephant would become sick and unable to regain its feet. One attempt after another would be made until eventually, after many years, the elephant would rise to its feet and remain on them for a number of years, but would then go down and the country with it. There would then follow an unprecedented period of war, confusion, turmoil, and national disaster.

SIZE OF MONEY REDUCED
Bishop Koyle saw and told this in the early twenties that they would cut down the size of the greenbacks. You'll remember we used to have greenbacks about one and one-half times the size of what they are today. The miner that he told this to kept one of the $5.00 bills, which is redeemable in gold.

GOLD IS CALLED IN
Bishop Koyle told the miners that worked for him in 1920 that the government would call in all the gold in not many years. Do you remember this happened in 1933?

STATE TO BE A PARTNER IN THE MINE

About 1930 it was made known to the Bishop that he would have a partner in the Mine. It happened the State of Utah traded a section of land down in the southern part of Utah to the Government for Section 16 which just happened to be 640 acres right over the richest part of the nine rooms. This will give Utah 12-1/2 per cent of all the gold taken out of that area without them working at all for it. In addition, they have been receiving $320 per year ever since then.

STREETCAR TRACKS IN SALT LAKE CITY

Koyle said that probably in the thirties the mine would come in after the streetcar tracks were taken up in Salt Lake City. They took them up in the year 1945, as near as I remember.

THIS IS ALL THAT WILL BE HERE

One Thursday night, just a few days before Christmas in 1943, eight men came down to the mine earlier than usual so they could visit with the Bishop before the meeting began. When time for the meeting arrived, the Bishop said, "We might as well get started--this is all that will be here." The others looked out the window and saw a string of car lights heading up towards the mine. They called this to the Bishop's attention, but he still maintained that there would be no more arrive for the meeting. The meeting commenced, and no one else came. Afterward, they bid goodbye to the Bishop and started down the hill. They saw the reason that no one came to the meeting--the wind had blown big snow drifts over the road. A snow plow was just clearing the road, but the cars had previously turned back, since it would have been too late to get to the meeting.

BEACON ON THE MOUNTAIN

Once the Bishop pointed to the top of the mountains and said that the day would come when a light would be seen up there. A few years after the Bishop's death, the telephone company came to the officials of the mine for permission to share the use of their dugway so that a tower could be placed atop the mountain for a coast to coast dial system. When the tower was completed, a large beacon light was placed on top which could be seen from anywhere in the valley.

THE DROUGHT OF 1938

The Bishop once prophesied that there would be a drought come to the intermountain region. Then one day in May of 1938, after many continuous days of raining, the miners were kidding the Bishop not to worry about a famine or drought, but rather consider building an ark if the rains continued any longer. The Bishop listened to their joking and then replied that the rains would stop the next day and the drought would begin. Sure enough, the rains stopped on May the 18th and no moisture came until October. And, for the next few years the drought continued.

WORLD WAR I FORETOLD

Another of these outstanding dreams with a very narrow margin of timing was one that Bishop Koyle had back in 1908 or 1909, when he foretold World War I, and how the United States would be involved. He told how it would strike home to us because the 145th Field Artillery of Utah boys would be called to the colors. However, that should not concern anyone very much because they would never see any action on the front lines.

HOUSES LIKE CHICKEN COOPS

The Bishop was amused at how some of the new houses would look at this time. He said that they seemed to be patterned after chicken coops. They would have almost flat roofs and a big window in front, and cost so much that the people who lived in them would be worried as to how they could ever pay for them. When we first heard this it seemed ridiculous that people would ever build houses like that. Shortly after World War II, new housing developments began to boom around the country building home exactly this way. This style is still current and so are the heavy mortgages.

A LONG AND A SHORT SHUT DOWN

Bishop Koyle occasionally spoke of a long shut down, and also a short shut down that the mine must experience before final vindication. Many of us thought that the long shut down must be the one in the past from 1914 to 1920; but history was to prove that it was yet in the future. He saw that the miners would leave the hill, even he would not be there. The stockholders would be at bitter logger-heads with each other, and some who had been the best of friends, now would be enemies. Two of the directors would turn their backs on the mine, while the others would not be of much use to it. Some of the stock would change hands for as little as ten cents a share, while others would even regard it as of no value at all. In fact, it would appear as though this whole project was at long last finished and dead, once and for all. For that matter, mining elsewhere in Utah would be dead or in a very dilapidated condition. He would point to the Tintic-Eureka district while saying this, indicating there would be little or no activity.

DARK, BLACK CLOUDS
The final struggle toward the end was further emphasized in another dream in which he saw heavy, dark, black clouds gather over the valley and weigh depressingly heavy over the mine until there appeared to be no hope for the mine at all. Everything seemed to be crushed out of existence and the whole thing had come to an end. The Dream Mine really appeared to be finished and ended.

MUDDY WATER IN THE STREETS LIKE RIVERS
While compiling information for the first edition of this book, Ogden Kruat noticed a prophecy attributed to Bishop Koyle that was recorded by Norman Pierce. Since Pierce was no longer alive for confirmation and since he personally had never heard Bishop Koyle give such a prophecy, he decided not to include it in his book. Furthermore, he thought it sounded too fantastic and impossible to ever be fulfilled.
Koyle told people, "It looks like it won't be long now before we'll be having some of the big troubles we've been expecting. I saw in a dream the other night that muddy water would flow in the streets like rivers in almost every community from one end of the state
to the other. When it comes, it's going to cause a lot of trouble for a lot of people around here. It will be the beginning of really big troubles."
In the spring of about 1951 we had a real river of about three feet deep running west on 13th South. The streetcars went across on a bridge that was elevated at least four feet. Both sides of the street were sandbagged to a height of about four feet. I saw a man in about an 18-foot boat going west from State Street.
Years later, in 1983, rains began to pour over the state of Utah. They continued until water literally ran down the streets of cities from one end of the state to the other. Some small towns were literally abandoned until the water receded. Over half of the counties asked for Federal Emergency Assistance. A river had overflowed it's banks and was running down Main Street contained by sandbags and people fishing in it in down town Salt Lake City.
The Agriculture and Health Committee was told that Utah's farms and ranches have sustained an estimated $57.7 million loss. (S.L. Tribune, "Utah Floods", p. 62)
There were $63 million dollars in road damages in the State. The total estimate for damages from the rains and too rapidly melting snow came to over $200 million dollars.

GENEVA STEEL, KENNECOTT UTAH COPPER AND TINTIC MINING DISTRICT
At a thursday night meeting the bishop told stockholders that a big employer in Salt Lake City, Kennecott Copper and a new modern steel plant built on the edge of the Utah Lake as a result of the war efforts in WW II, Geneva Steel, would both close down toward the end times. This happened about 40 years later. First Kennecott shut down it's Bingham Canyon operation in Utah and then Geneva Steel followed suit soon after. They both reopened their doors within a couple of years with Geneva reopening with new owners. Geneva closed once again due to cheap foreign steel imports and presently (2004), Kennecott is wondering they will be around in the next few years.

Koyle also said that when the mine came in, all the mines in Tintic District in Utah would be at a stand still. This is pretty much the case today.

A WARNING ABOUT WALL STREET RIGHT BEFORE THE FINAL CRASH

Bishop Koyle said that Wall Street would have a major drop sometime before the total failure and that the Government would step in to help save it. In October 1988 (Black Monday) the stock market came to within two hours of total catastrophe and the federal government stepped in to prevent it from crashing. Then again on 11 September 2001 when the twin towers of the Trade Center came crashing down, the markets took a big tumble when they reopened for business. On his radio talk show, G. Gordon Liddy reported that a friend of his working for Merrill Lynch, a stock brokerage firm, called to tell him that the government was feeding funds into the market.

CHURCH, STATE AND NATION

Koyle said also the Church, the State, and the Nation, in rapid succession would be set in order and brought up a standin' like a wild colt to the snubbing post.

A SEVEN YEAR SCOURGE OF DROUGHT

Associated with this time of distress and one of the principal things that would compound it beyond endurance for many, was a four year drought, attended by great crop failures and famine, which would require from two to three years for recovery, depending upon where one lived. There would be seven distressful years filled and compounded with drought, plague, famine, warfare, and other divine judgments that would sweep the wicked from off the face of the earth in preparation of the Lord's second coming. He had a favorite expression to characterize these events when he would say: "A setting-in-order will take place, and the Church, the State and the Nation will be brought up a standin' to judgment like a wild colt to a snubin' post." Yes, there would be a setting-in-order develop right along the line to prepare the whole earth for the coming of Christ. It was like going down into a deep valley that would take 3 1/2 years to go down into, and another 3 1/2 years to climb out again into a new and wonderful world.

He always described this series of drought years and crop shortages as follows: The first year would not be felt very much; but the second year would be worse with less crops; and the third year would also produce very poor crops; and in the fourth year there would be no crops at all.

In the fourth year he saw the grain come up around here like it was going to make into a bumper crop, and then something made it all wither and die like a blight or a terrific heat had taken it, leaving the people without harvest and in famine. And there was famine all over the country, not only because of these crop shortages, but because of the great troubles that had come causing manufacturing and transportation to cease. In fact, he saw that, although we had plenty of gold available, try as we would everywhere, we could buy no wheat with it.

Further, that in the fifth year, there would be plenty of moisture again but there would still be a shortage of food in the land because of the lack of seed to plant, --most of the seed having been eaten for food. And that only after the harvest of the sixth year, and in some places not until after the harvest of the seventh year, would crop production revert to abundance.

Some have quoted Bishop Koyle as describing the progress of the drought years about as follows: The first year,-- about a seventy-five percent crop; the second year,--about a fifty percent crop; the third year,--about a twenty-five percent crop; the fourth year, no crops at all.
He pointed out that we should secure our wheat from the first and second years, because that raised in the third year would not be fit for human consumption because of its very poor quality; and in the fourth year there was no grain to be purchased at any price.

When these years arrived, he said, there would be very little doubt as to their being the right years, for RELIEF would be the biggest and most important issue of the day. As time went on, we would be reluctant to listen to the news, because it would all be so awful distressing and vexing that we would prefer not to hear about it.

A LITTLE PATCH OF BLUE

When it seemed as if all was lost and the Dream Mine had come to complete failure, he looked from the mine, while standing on Knob Hill, over to the northwest toward the Point-of-the-Mountain and beheld a small rift in the dark clouds revealing a little spot of blue about the size of a man's hand. As he watched it, this rift suddenly expanded, and with a majestic sweep, the heavens were cleared of the dark, black, oppressive clouds, and the mine and its surroundings were restored to the brilliant sunshine of a fine, glorious day, with all oppressiveness having vanished away.

THE MINE COMES IN
He also saw the Mine would come in after a hard winter followed by a water-logged spring, then a dry hot summer, and when the wheat was in the boot, the Bishop came out of the tunnel with the first gold in his hands.

THE LIGHT COMPLEXIONED - WHITE HAIRED MAN
When it was time for the mine to turn out, he said, there was a light complexioned man with white hair who would come from east of the mine with a big check to finance the first shipment of ore. He seemed to be identified with "the little spot of blue in the dark clouds over by the Point of the Mountain." In one or two rounds of holes they would strike the rich gold ore in the fourth finger of the five fingers in the right-hand drift. The stockholders would rally with him and bring about many wonderful changes around the mine. This man would come with a new process that would entirely revolutionize the entire mining industry. Could this man be Al Sinclair AKA as the translated Alma the Younger who came to the mine in the 1950's? the Bishop along with Al Sinclair said that the messengers would return before the mine opened in their true identity. Al had a lot of interest in new inventions and mining. Who would know best how things should be done when the mine is to be opened.

WAR COMES TO OUR COAST LINE
War would be brought to our coast line, but we would not be invaded at this time. However, a Russian invasion of the U.S. and Canada would come later.

FUTURE OVERNITE CRASH / U.S. PRESIDENT TO DIE
One time in about 1946 an attorney who was quite interested in the Mine, and sometimes he attended the Thursday night meetings, said to the Bishop, "How are you going to stop the Government from taking about 94% of the gold away from you?" The Bishop said, "Turney, there ain't goin' to be no Government when the Mine comes in!"

Bishop Koyle said that on the first shipment of gold that there would be a small piece in the paper near the mining page and few people would see it. It would be about one inch long in the paper. At this same date and on this same paper there would be four-inch headlines. We were never told what those headlines would be about. Also, when the second shipment of gold was made, there would be a jam at the mountain and hundreds of people would never get up there to be in the midst of it. I understood this jam would reach for several miles.

Koyle saw that the US President would die in office just a while after the mine came in. He saw them look up and down the country everywhere to try to find a man to take his place and they would not be able to find one and the nation wandered in chaos. That's how bad it will get.

He was shown that a Republican Administration would made great efforts to save the economy. He also said prices would go higher and higher and all at once something happened and in one night the props would be knocked out from under everything and down would come everything. This condition of rising prices would be brought about by strikes.

When the props give away there will suddenly be an overnight price and wage crash or deflation that seemed to occur the same time as the death of the republican president. The disaster which followed rated 4-inch headlines in newspapers throughout the country.

According to Velma Kunz who was the wife of a miner that lived on the hill near the mine, the bishop would many times get the miners off to work and then come on down the hill. He would many times stop in and talk to Velma. One day she asked when the economic crash would occur. He was sitting at the time with his arms across his chest and then he dropped his head down. She thought he had gone to sleep. After a period of time he opened his eyes and looked up at her and told her this. The overnite crash would occur on a holiday weekend where the holiday falls on a Monday.

Koyle was shown that our entire wage and price structure had risen higher and higher so that it was like it was up on high stilts, and then suddenly it was as if someone over-night had kicked the stilts out from under it, and the whole thing came down with a crash to about 20 cents on the dollar.

Property would only be worth l/5 of its form er value, but his mortgage and other fixed debts would remain the same.

The US would call it's military home from all over the world just to keep the greenbacks home and to keep the peace.

CHURCHES AND SCHOOLS TO CLOSE
Bishop saw that after the Mine came in, that all the churches and schools would be closed down for a while. He saw this in about 1930.

U.S. MONEY TO BECOME WORTHLESS
Additionally Koyle said, not long after the mine came in, the U.S. money would become totally worthless.

THE MINE TURNS OUT IN THE FALL
A small notice would appear in the paper about the mine shipping it's first shipment of ore to be processed but the biggest economic disaster in the world would be the news of the day and would affect everyone.

The mine would pay it's first dividends or relief from the mine in November or December. Koyle said he had a dream that after the mine came in, many were sitting around and giving praise to God for this happy Christmas. In time we would learn to live without money under the Law of Consecration.

The Bishop said probably in the thirties that when the Mine comes in, we will have a queer lot of Dream Miners that want to do many things. One would buy a large automobile and tour many countries in the world; many would buy large ranches and stock them well with cattle; and Parley here would charter a ship and go down into Central America and hire a lot of men and uncover one of those ancient temples, and bring his findings back and give them to the BYU.

THE MOST IMPORTANT THING TO DO
Well now, Bishop Koyle will tell you the most important thing for you to do. You should have your houses filled with a large amount of food, and go inside and cut off your radio, TV, your telephone, and your daily papers. You will not want to know what is going on in the outside world at all. I saw that two out of every three people on the earth would lose their lives from starving, or from being killed on account of the judgments of God that would be in full swing. I saw that I could walk great distances right here in Utah, by stepping from one man's dead body to the other. After you get inside your houses, you will be in there for quite some time. To me, my own opinion would be we would be there for the third and fourth years of famine, and probably another one because there was such a shortage of seeds to plant that there was not an abundance until the sixth year. I have been wrong before, and the best thing to do is to pray to Him for advice.

MEN OFFER TO BUY THE MINE
Bishop Koyle said that right after the Mine came in, there would be two men from the east, and they would bring suitcases filled with gold, and stack it on the dining room table in great stacks, and offer it all to the Bishop for his Mine. The Bishop only smiled and said, "No."
The Bishop said that if people could travel very far, this being the richest gold mine in the entire world anywhere, there would be many whores, gamblers, drunkards, confidence men, and what have you. All of them would be trying to make a stake for themselves. God will not permit this on His works.

$6,000 PER SHARE

Bishop said this stock would go to a high of $6,000 per share, and he saw that people would go to court for one-half of one share.

A SILVER DOLLAR WILL BUY ONE ACRE OF LAND

The bishop made the comment many times at the Thursday night meetings that the day would come when a silver dollar would buy an acre of land.

THE PURPOSE OF THIS GREAT WEALTH

The purpose of this great wealth was that it must be reserved for building the nucleus for the political Kingdom of God. It would provide an honest money of gold and silver the would make possible the rapid construction of cities of refuge and stock them with food supplies and equip them with essential industries, so that these cities could be a refuge for righteous populations which would be segregated out in fulfillment of the parable of the wheat and the tares, thereby bringing to pass "an entire separation of the righteous from the wicked," as stated in D&C,63:54, and also in Section 86. This gold would also serve a wonderful purpose in beautifying the New Jerusalem and the Great Temple to be built there for the Lord's coming. A City to be inhabited by Nephites, Lamanites, the Ten Lost Tribes, and the repentant LDS Gentiles then sifted out.

GRAIN BINS TO BE BUILT

Carter Grant recorded some of his conversations with Bishop Koyle on these important matters:

Wednesday, March 4, 1931:

Last night Brothers William A. Jones, Clyde Hood, Philip Tadje, Richard Sonntag, and I went to Brother Koyle's, arriving at 8:00 p.m. After asking each one of us about the hard times, getting what we knew, Brother Koyle opened declaring that they would grow worse and worse each week; that even the Church would become so hard pressed that the cry of the needy could not be satisfied.

Also he said, "We will have a mild open winter after the mine comes in, which will permit us to pour concrete all winter long to build the grain bins He spoke of a fall following the dry, hot summer that would be more like spring when the mine turned out, and it would be followed by a very mild, open winter which would permit the uninterrupted construction of a series of large grain bins, or elevators which would hold a million bushels of wheat. These would be built high on the hill near the mine and get them filled up against this time of great distress and famine. These would hold one million bushels of grain. This we would do, he said, barely in the nick-of-time before it would be too late when no more food supplies could be purchased at any price. This would keep many, many thousands of people from starving during the time of famine. At the very same time, he saw that the 315,000 [bushel] grain elevator built at Welfare Square in Salt Lake City would be entirely empty right at the time it would be most needed.

March 14, 1931:

Now as to storing wheat! Since this subject has been upon Brother Koyle's mind for some time, he stated to us that on Friday, March 13th, while coming out the tunnel, inspiration came to him like a voice speaking, telling him to build double cement bins on the side hill near the powder magazine, one below the other, so that he could let the grain from the first bin run down into the next and then down into the third and fourth. These long cement tanks or bins were to begin at the upper road and stretch down the hill, so that with the gates open between the bins, grain that was dropped into the top one would easily find its way down the incline to the lowest level. * * * Then too, this plan, says Bishop Koyle, "will put the grain upon our property where no one can molest it, where we can make distribution as we see fit. All eyes are to look toward us for relief."

(Journal of Carter Grant)

He urged us to look forward to the fifth year, when a great change would take place in the earth and it would be much different so that "the former rains and the latter rains would return moderately," and the earth would no longer be a thirsty land, but would yield richly from its seed. It would only be because of a shortage of seed that we must still eat sparingly.

He also saw that we would buy our wheat at 50 to 60 cents per bushel, and that it would be bought out of the first and second years of crops in those famine years. He looked up and down the state everywhere on the third year of famine, and he could not buy a bushel of wheat for a bushel of gold.

We learned through the Bishop we would have nine months to build grain bins and store food, and that would be the longest that money would be good until transportation fails.

INDUSTRY AND BUSINESS CLOSE

Here in Utah, big industries would be shut down as well as government related industries and unemployment would be widespread.

GREAT EARTHQUAKES

John H. Koyle was gifted with dreams not directly related to the mine. For example, he saw that during the time of great tribulation there would be a massive earthquake out in the Pacific Ocean that would bring giant tidal waves along our Pacific Coast. This would in turn bring destructive quakes along the San Andreas Fault and wreck great destruction in San Francisco and Oakland. If inspired, prophetic warnings were heeded in time, many of our people would escape these disasters.

DROUGHT, FAMINE AND DEATH

The Bishop said we would have four years of famine here in Utah due to a 4-year drought and increasing crop failures. The last two years of this would result in major famine, causing many to die of hunger and plague. Overall, there would be seven years of famine in the world. The fifth year here would be ever so scarce because of a shortage of seeds to plant. The sixth year the rains came and there would be an abundance from then on. One third of the people is all that would enjoy it as the rest would be dead.

The time would come when one could not buy a bushel of wheat for a bushel of gold, but during those first two years of the drought, wheat could be purchased for as little as 50 and 60 cents a bushel; and thus from our gold and silver we would be able to get enough to survive the famine here in these valleys.

REFUGES AND TENT CITIES

The nation was in a sad state of famine, mobocracy and chaos exactly as seen and prophesied by the Prophet Joseph Smith. Entire states would be depopulated, with not enough living to bury the dead. This in turn would cause a great influx of tens of thousands refugees, consisting mostly of women and children, looking for food and safety until there were more people living in tents than in houses in the valleys of Utah. The Bishop also said that two out of every three would die or be killed when the judgments of God came, and this would be true all around the entire world.

TRANSPORTATION TO STOP

We would have our gold and be able to buy our food and grain supplies barely in the nick-of-time he said, because in a short time the situation would grow so bad that all of the automobiles and trains would stop running, and manufacturing would cease because of a complete breakdown in our economy. They would have to put the horseless carriage back in the barn and get the horse out, if they still had a horse. (He made this prediction so far back that the terms "Automobile" and "garage" were not yet in popular usage.)

Back in the early part of the century, when the automobile was still a novelty, he would tell his listeners that these vehicles would be so numerous before long, that almost everybody would have one and they would get to be as big as boxcars, and be filled with people going at great speeds up and down the highways, and they would drive thru the night with brilliant lights. Soon they would be lined up so thick along the curb on business streets, that it would be difficult for one to get from the street into the stores and back again. Of course, no one in the early part of the century believed him.

About this time, he said, transportation would stop all over the country, and manufacturing would cease, and the people would have to return to their horses, if they had any, or go on foot. Then we could no longer buy any wheat because there was no way to get to where the big supplies were located, nor could it be brought to us. And those who did have any wheat on hand would not sell it for a bushel of gold. Then the really big troubles began with famine, warfare, plagues and judgments, and we would have to make White City and the Dream Mine into a fortress to protect ourselves from ravaging mobs. In many places, he said, the dead would outnumber the living, while in others there would not even be enough living to bury the dead. We would have to build a self-sufficient economy of our own with oil wells and industries to take care of our own needs. This, indeed, would be a time when we would have to live close to the Lord and depend upon Him for both temporal and spiritual salvation. We would learn the meaning of repentance.

WHITE CITY, A CITY OF REFUGE

The Bishop explained that a beautiful city would grow at the base of the mountain after the mine came in. Nearly all of the people of the city would be stockholders, or at least believe in the mission of the mine. So many of the buildings would be painted white, that it would be called "White City".

When Ogden Kraut went to work at the mine, he met an elderly gentleman named Salsbury, who had been a barber in California before being employed at the mine. He told me that while they were living in California, he came home one day after work and lay down on the living room couch to rest. His wife asked him if he would like to go with her to the store, but he declined by saying he would rather just rest for awhile. After she left, he was looking over towards the wall when suddenly it began to vanish, but a vision of a beautiful valley came into view. He saw mountains in the background and a large lake nearby. He was high in the air looking down, and there below him was a beautiful city in which almost every building was painted white. He looked upon the scene with awe and wonderment, when suddenly the picture began to fade away and the wall came back into view. He was puzzled as to what it was, what it meant, and where the valley was. For over a year he marveled at the beautiful scene that he had beheld in vision.

Then one day he went to Utah to visit some relatives who lived in Provo. During the visit they mentioned the Dream Mine, and how spiritual the Bishop was. They all agreed that it would be a very interesting visit to go up to the mine to see it. Salsbury went into the tunnel on their little guided tour and was utterly fascinated. Finally, on his exit from the main tunnel, he beheld mountains, the lake and the beautiful valley below--it was just as he had seen it in his vision, except there was no city below the hill. He hurried down to the house where the Bishop was and asked him what had happened to all the buildings that were supposed to be there. The Bishop told him that he had seen the city that would someday be built there.

White City would become one of many cities to spring up in the valleys of the Rocky Mountains. It would be designated along with others, as a place of refuge, a place of safety and peace from the scourges that would overtake the fallen nations of the world:

This beautiful "White City" together with a number of other beautiful cities, were to be rapidly built at this time and would serve as holy places of refuge where the more righteous of the LDS could be gathered out for safety as in the parable of the wheat and the tares, a people who would be determined to accept a Great Reformation that would be offered to them at this time, and they would dedicate themselves to living the Gospel of Jesus Christ in all its fullness with nothing left out. There would be radio and TV stations, power plants and airports arise in these ultra modern cities, and they would be stocked with food and equipped with essential industries that would enable them to survive the years of famine and distress, while the Lord purged the earth in preparation for His Millennial Reign. Here the very elect of the earth would prepare themselves to pioneer the New Age with a New Society that would replace the fallen Babylon. (The Dream Mine Story, Pierce, p. 64)

TO COME US ARMY

In 1934 construction began on the dugway that winds up the side of the mountain from the mill and over the saddle, linking the various tunnels together on the upper claims. This dugway would someday prove to have greater additional importance for the inhabitants of White City during a time of grave danger. Bishop Koyle saw that it would serve them as a means to places of refuge and safety where they could take needed supplies with them and find protection from an invading U.S. Army, larger than was Johnston's Army sent against the Saints about a century ago, This army would have orders to destroy them if they did not surrender and deny all affiliation with the new parliamentary nation.

While working on the Dream Mine dugway, June 17, 1934, I was standing with a pick on my shoulder talking to Bishop John H. Koyle, when the spirit of prophecy came over him, and pointing to me, he said, "Just as sure as you stand there with that pick on your shoulder, the time will come when you young men will have to defend this land against factions that will come here against us. You will defend it by the power of the Priesthood.

"They will send an army out here worse than Johnston's Army to put us down. They will offer protection to all who will deny their faith and surrender to them. And all the Gentiles will go over to them and about one third of the Mormons. Then when they are ready to completely destroy those of us who defy them, something will prevent them from doing it.

"During that time this dugway will serve as a means to refuge for many of our people with their supplies. We take cover in the safety of the tunnels until that army is destroyed together with all who surrender.

"Following this, we will also have the Russians to fight, and they will get half way across this country before they are put down." (--To the Missouri River.)

I noticed that he was somewhat shaken by this experience, and that he had to sit down to recover his strength. Later when I had discovered the Bulkley and Farnsworth visions about the U.S. Army coming against Zion, I learned that Bishop Koyle had never heard of them, and that he had no previous knowledge of the "U.S. Army worse than Johnston's coming against Utah."

When he had recovered enough to talk about it, I then pointed out that the tunnels would not offer much protection against an army. He then told me that the importance of the tunnels would be understood when this time came. Of course, I did not know in 1934, as I know today, that we would be taking refuge from the wrath of God upon the army and all who would surrender to it, when "the heavens being on fire shall be dissolved, and the elements shall melt with fervent heat." (II Peter, 3:12) And "the light of the moon shall be as the light of the sun, and the light of the sun shall be sevenfold." (See Isaiah, 30:26.)

Oddly enough, a dugway that was constructed in 1934, many years after the dream was given, divided the ravine in which the main tunnel is located, into three segments; a short one, a long one, and another short one. And in like manner the history of the mine may be divided into three sections:--a relatively short one from 1894 to 1914, free from any troublesome opposition; --then a long one from 1914 to 1949, the time of Bishop Koyle's death, which was a long period of 35 years full of all manner of opposition from the Church, State, and Nation; and then the third period from his death to the present time, during which the mine has been rather dormant with little more than enough activity to justify the assessment work and keep a legal hold on the claims. The full symbolic vindication of the Green Spot is now due.

(parts of this vision have been removed for space consideration)

Awesome Preparedness Quotes from LDS Church Leaders

"We urge all Latter-day Saints to be prudent in their planning, to be conservative in their living, and to avoid excessive or unnecessary debt." – President Thomas S. Monson, October 2008 Priesthood Session, General Conference

"Avoid the philosophy that yesterday's luxuries have become today's necessities. They aren't necessities until we make them so. Many enter into long-term debt only to find that changes occur; people become ill or incapacitated, companies fail or downsize, jobs are lost, natural disasters befall us. For many reasons, payments on large amounts of debt can no longer be made. Our debt becomes as a Damocles sword hanging over our heads and threatening to destroy us."

- President Thomas S. Monson, April 2006 General Conference

"We have built grain storage and storehouses and stocked them with the necessities of life in the event of a disaster. But the real storehouse is the family storeroom. In words of revelation the Lord has said, 'Organize yourselves; prepare every needful thing' (D&C 109:8.)"

President Gordon B. Hinckley

"We need to make both temporal and spiritual preparation for the events prophesied at the time of the Second Coming. And the preparation most likely to be neglected is the one less visible and more difficult–the spiritual. A 72-hour kit of temporal supplies may prove valuable for earthly challenges, but, as the foolish virgins learned to their sorrow, a 24-hour kit of spiritual preparation is of greater and more enduring value.

"We are living in the prophesied time 'when peace shall be taken from the earth' (D&C 1:35,) when 'all things shall be in commotion' and 'men's hearts shall fail them' (D&C 88:91.) There are many temporal causes of commotion, including wars and natural disasters, but an even greater cause of current 'commotion' is spiritual." Elder Dallin H. Oaks

"Every father and mother are the family's store keepers. They should store whatever their family would like to have in case of an emergency…(and) God will sustain us through our trials." President James E. Faust

"Many more people could ride out the storm-tossed waves in their economic lives if they had their year's supply of food. . . and were debt-free. Today we find that many have followed this counsel in reverse: they have at least a year's supply of debt and are food free." President Thomas S. Monson

"Just as it is important to prepare ourselves spiritually, we must also prepare ourselves for our temporal needs. … We have been instructed for years to follow at least four requirements in preparing for that which is to come.

"First, gain an adequate education. Learn a trade or a profession to enable you to obtain steady employment that will provide remuneration sufficient to care for yourself and your family. …

"Second, live strictly within your income and save something for a rainy day. Incorporate in your lives the discipline of budgeting that which the Lord has blessed you with. As regularly as you pay your tithing, set aside an amount needed for future family requirements. …

"Third, avoid excessive debt. Necessary debt should be incurred only after careful, thoughtful prayer and after obtaining the best possible advice. We need the discipline to stay well within our ability to pay. …

"Fourth, acquire and store a reserve of food and supplies that will sustain life [if local laws permit such storage]. Obtain clothing and build a savings account on a sensible, well-planned basis that can serve well in times of emergency. As long as I can remember, we have been taught to prepare for the future and to obtain a year's supply of necessities. I would guess that the years of plenty have almost universally caused us to set aside this counsel. I believe the time to disregard this counsel is over. With events in the world today, it must be considered with all seriousness." – Elder L. Tom Perry, October 1995 General Conference

"Maintain a year's supply. The Lord has urged that his people save for the rainy days, prepare for the difficult times, and put away for emergencies, a year's supply or more of bare necessities so that when comes the flood, the earthquake, the famine, the hurricane, the storms of life, our families can be sustained through the dark days. How many of us have complied with this? We strive with the Lord, finding many excuses: We do not have room for storage. The food spoils. We do not have the funds to do it. We do not like these common foods. It is not needed — there will always be someone to help in trouble. The government will come to the rescue. And some intend to obey but procrastinate." – The Teachings of Spencer W. Kimball, p.375

"All too often a family's spending is governed more by their yearning than by their earning. They somehow believe that their life will be better if they surround themselves with an abundance of things. All too often all they are left with is avoidable anxiety and distress" – Elder Joseph B. Wirthlin

"Be prepared in all things against the day when tribulations and desolations are sent forth upon the wicked." D&C 29:8

"Too often we bask in our comfortable complacency and rationalize that the ravages of war, economic disaster, famine, and earthquake cannot happen here. Those who believe this are either not acquainted with the revelations of the Lord, or they do not believe them." President Ezra Taft Benson

"Fear not little flock; do good; let earth and hell combine against you, for if ye are built upon my rock, they cannot prevail. . .Look unto me in every thought; doubt not, fear not." D&C 6:34, 36

"I believe that the Ten Virgins represent the people of the Church of Jesus Christ. . . They (five foolish) had the saving, exalting gospel, but it had not been made the center of their lives. They knew the way but gave only a small measure of loyalty and devotion.

"The foolish asked the others to share their oil, but spiritual preparedness cannot be shared in an instant. . . . This was not selfishness or unkindness. The kind of oil that is needed to illuminate the way and light up the darkness is not shareable. . . . In our lives the oil of preparedness is accumulated drop by drop in righteous living." – President Spencer W. Kimball

"We encourage families to have on hand this year's supply; we say it over and over and over and repeat over and over the scripture of the Lord where he says, "Why call ye me, Lord, Lord and do not the things which I say?" How empty it is as they put their spirituality, so-called, into action and call him by his important names, but fail to do the things which he says." – President Spencer W. Kimball

"I stand before the Church this day and raise the warning voice. It is a prophetic voice, for I shall say only what the apostles and the prophets have spoken concerning our day. …It is a voice calling upon the Lord's people to prepare for the troubles and desolations which are about to be poured upon the world without measure. For the moment, we live in a day of peace and prosperity but it shall not ever be thus. Great trials lie ahead. All of the sorrows and perils of the past are but a foretaste of what is yet to be. And we must prepare ourselves temporally and spiritually." – Bruce R. McConkie (General Conference April 1979)

"Let every head of every household see to it that he has on hand enough food and clothing, and, where possible, fuel also, for at least a year ahead" – J. Reuben Clark (General Conference April 1937.)

"Should the Lord decide at this time to cleanse the Church … a famine in this land of one year's duration could wipe out a large percentage of sloughful members, including some ward and stake officers. Yet we cannot say we have not been warned." – Ezra Taft Benson (General Conference, April 1965)

"For the righteous, the gospel provides a warning before calamity, a program for the crises, refuge for each disaster… The Lord has warned us of famines, but the righteous will have listened to the prophets and stored at least one year's supply of survival food…"- Ezra Taft Benson (General Conference, October 1973)

"The little gardens and a few trees are very valuable. I remember when the sisters used to say, `well, but we could buy it at the store a lot cheaper than we could put it up.' But that isn't quite the answer, is it, Sister Spafford? Because there will become a time when there isn't a store."- Spencer W. Kimball (General Conference, April 1974)

"On the average, about 30 percent of the church has a two-month supply of food. The remainder have little or none…become self-sufficient as possible to prepare against the days to come."- Bishop H. Burke Peterson (General Conference October 1975)

"Plan to build up your food supply just as you would a savings account… We urge you to do this prayerfully and do it now." – Ezra Taft Benson (General Conference, October 1980)

"We feel the need to emphasize with greater clarity the obligation for members of the Church to become more independent and self reliant." – Gordon B. Hinckley (General Conference, April 1983)

"Plan to build up your food supply just as you would a savings account… We urge you to do this prayerfully and do it now." – Ezra Taft Benson (General Conference, October 1980)

"Noah heeded God's command to build an ark…that they might be saved from the floodwaters. Yet there was no evidence of rain and flood. His actions were considered irrational. The sun was shining and life moved forward as usual. But time ran out. The floods came, the disobedient were drowned. When God speaks and we obey, we will always be right." – Thomas S. Monson (October 2002 Ensign)

"Will you be slack, brethren, and let the evil come upon us, when we forewarn you of the future events that are coming;… We are telling of what the prophets have said-of what the Lord has said to Joseph. Wake up now, wake up, O Israel, and lay up your grain and your stores. I tell you that there is trouble coming upon the world…" – Heber C. Kimball (Journal of Discourses, vol. 4, p. 336-9)

"A great many have taken this counsel, and they are prepared…Who is deserving of praise? The persons who take care of themselves, or the ones who always trust in the great mercies of the Lord to take care of them? It is just as consistent to expect that the Lord will supply us with fruit when we do not plant the trees; or that, when we do not plow and sow and are saved the labor of harvesting, we should cry to the Lord to save us from want, as to ask Him to save us from the consequences of our own folly, disobedience and waste…"The Lord has said, 'Gather and save the produce I put within your reach, and prepare against a day of want."- Brigham Young (Journal of Discourses, vol. 12, p. 244)

Preparedness is Two Pronged

By Shelle McDermott as a guest blogger for DIYPreparedness.com, 2015

Many *preppers* are busily storing up for a future time when resources will be scarce, but is that enough to get us through long periods of hardship? Church leaders tell us there is something else equally important to your supplies - ***spiritual preparedness.***

Here's a quote from *A 72-hour kit of temporal supplies may prove valuable for earthly challenges, but, as the foolish virgins learned to their sorrow, a 24-hour kit of spiritual preparation is of greater and more enduring value".*

With all the chatter and physical prepping going on, a key element to surviving the chaos and calamities lies in the scriptures and modern day prophets. Physical preparedness and spiritual preparedness must go together.

Physical preparations should be an outward sign of obedience to your spiritual preparedness, otherwise we become just another a *doomsday prepper* with more ammo and food than humility and charity. When we arm ourselves temporally and not spiritually, we miss the mission of ushering in the Millennium.

President Spencer W. Kimball shares how spiritual preparedness is obtained:

"I believe that the Ten Virgins represent the people of the Church of Jesus Christ. . . They (five foolish) had the saving, exalting gospel, but it had not been made the center of their lives. They knew the way but gave only a small measure of loyalty and devotion.

"The foolish asked the others to share their oil, but spiritual preparedness cannot be shared in an instant. . . . This was not selfishness or unkindness. The kind of oil that is needed to illuminate the way and light up the darkness is not shareable. . . . In our lives the oil of preparedness is accumulated drop by drop in righteous living."

How can we prepare spiritually?

1. <u>Have consistent Family Home Evening and Family Council.</u>

We learn from **President Gordon B. Hinckley:** *"We have built grain storage and storehouses and stocked them with the necessities of life in the event of a disaster. But the real storehouse is the family storeroom. In words of revelation the Lord has said, 'Organize yourselves; prepare every needful thing' (D&C 109:8.)"*

It is essential that we build close family relationships, forgive one another, serve one another and support one another. Under pressure from challenges we often do not show our best side, yet if we build up our families now we will fare much better in future challenges.

2. <u>Stand in Holy Places.</u> It will be imperative that we can hear what the Lord needs to tell us during difficult times. We learn from **Elder Dallin H. Oaks:**

What are those "holy places"? Surely they include the temple and its covenants faithfully kept. Surely they include a home where children are treasured and parents are respected. Surely the holy places include our posts of duty assigned by priesthood authority, including missions and callings faithfully fulfilled in branches, wards, and stakes. Dallin H. Oaks

The Saints have been promised that we will gather as a people to endure the hardships together. It is imperative we are surrounding ourselves with activities that will allow us to hear the directive from the leadership when the call comes to gather.

Elder H. Aldridge (Second Quorum of the Seventy) LDS Business College Devotional, February 8th, 2005

"We must both learn what these signs are and then identify them correctly when they occur. They can and will strengthen our faith in Christ and His prophets, if we know the scriptures."
Just as in the days of Noah, a way is already prepared for the escape of the Lord's elect Latter-Day Saints, if they are in tune with His prophets."

3. <u>Follow the prophet, get out of debt.</u> Not only are we given specific instructions as how to prepare, obedience to each of these commands gives us spiritual strength.

President Thomas S. Monson reminds us:

"Avoid the philosophy that yesterday's luxuries have become today's necessities. They aren't necessities until we make them so. Many enter into long-term debt only to find that changes occur; people become ill or incapacitated, companies fail or downsize, jobs are lost, natural disasters befall us. For many reasons, payments on large amounts of debt can no longer be made. Our debt becomes as a Damocles sword hanging over our heads and threatening to destroy us."

When we are in debt, it makes it harder to prepare for physical preparations, we lose our peace worrying about the payment of our debts. Debt robs us of self-discipline.

4. <u>Increase our faith in Christ.</u> We are not to fear if we have been watching and preparing. We learn in D&C 6:34,36:

"Fear not little flock; do good; let earth and hell combine against you, for if ye are built upon my rock, they cannot prevail. . .Look unto me in every thought; doubt not, fear not."

Our burdens seem light, our disappointments seem manageable, and our pain seems qualified when we have developed a personal relationship with the Savior and know where to find him and how to feel his love.

5. <u>Increase our service to others.</u> Service changes people. It refines, purifies, gives a finer perspective, and brings out the best in each one of us. Righteous service is the expression of true charity, such as the Savior showed.

The duties of ushering in the Millennium will include gathering in many during the calamities and tribulations and caring for their physical and spiritual needs.

President Dieter F. Uchtdorf spoke of the apostle Paul's dramatic conversion and warned Latter-day Saints to not "spend their days waiting on the road to Damascus" but instead increase belief one step at a time, to hearken and heed, to serve others and to share the gospel.

"God loves you. He hears your prayers. He speaks to his children and offers comfort, peace and understanding to those who seek him and honor him by walking in his way," he said, adding "Let us not wait too long on our road to Damascus; let us courageously move forward in faith, hope and charity, and we will be blessed to discover the light we are all seeking on the path of discipleship."

We have been warned by modern prophets for a season now that we are preparing for Christ's coming. We will need our spiritual eyes to see, we will need our spiritual ears to hear so we can be guided how to prepare, when to prepare and what to prepare to usher in the Millennium. We will need to be refined and spiritually prepared through the tribulation period in order for us to be ready to meet the Savior at his coming.

Suggested Buckets & Bins List

Most of prepping is organizing what we already have. Here is a list of items that would be good in an emergency, calamity, or a gathering. Label buckets and when the time comes, gather and pack them if you have not already.

BUCKETS & BINS
Buckets are white, round, can be sealed tight, 5 gallons
Bins have lids, vary in size, stackable

Dishes: plates, bowls, silverware
Prepping Dishes: large bowls, spoons, spatulas, rubber scrapers, whisks, measuring cups
Pans: Dutch oven, iron skillet
Spice Bucket: spices, gravy mix, baking soda, yeast, bullion
Food Buckets: 72-hour emergency meals (1 bucket per family member)
Water Bottles: one case per family member
Disease Control Buckets: toilet seat/toilet paper
Shower Bucket: Solar shower bag, bar soap, face cloth, lotion, shaver, towels
Tool Bucket: Spare tools, hammer, screw driver, measure tape, glue
Quarantine Bucket: disposable overalls, gloves, masks (must have to treat sick people)
Laundry Bucket: plunger, soap, line and clothes pins
Cleaning Bucket: Scrubbers, cloths, soap, aprons, hand towels, all-purpose cleaner
Utility Bucket: tape, bungees, cutters, rope, wire, glue
Fuel Bucket: propane stove, 1lb propane bottles
First Aid Bucket: ointment, bandages, medications, braces, stomach ailments, flu remedies
Hygiene Bucket: shampoo/conditioner, toothpaste, make-up, q-tips, lotion, poison ivy lotion
Long term emergencies:
Sewing Bucket: thread, needles, scraps of material
Candle Bucket: left over candles, new candles, bag of wicks, matches
CD/DVD Bucket: personal DVD player, Uplifting DVD's, Music on iPod.
Library Bucket: books, scriptures
Game Bucket: cards, dominos, dice, chess
Baby Bucket: cloth diapers, bottles, blankets, pins
Military Bucket: binoculars, netting, ammo belt, knives, radio, 2-way radios
Office Bucket: paper, notebooks, pens, pencils, crayons
Weapons Bucket: guns, ammo, stun guns, etc.
Money Bucket: precious metals, cash, copies of family papers, passports, etc.
Clothing Bins:
Winter Clothing: overalls, gloves, beanies, cap, long underwear, wool socks, long sleeve t's, long sleeve shirts, jeans, coat, sweatshirts, vest
Summer Clothing: swimsuit (showers), shorts/capris, short sleeve shirts, sunglasses, socks, underwear, belt, hat/visor
Shoe Bucket: Boots, flip flops, sandals, tennis shoes
Bedding Bin: sleeping bag, wool blanket, pillow, camp blanket
To find out what your family weight limits are:

Food Storage your family will need:

Grains		
Wheat	600	lbs
Flour	98	lbs
Corn Meal	98	lbs
Oats	98	lbs
Rice	200	lbs
Pasta	98	lbs
Total Grains	1192	lbs

Sugars		
Honey	10	lbs
Sugar	160	lbs
Brown Sugar	10	lbs
Molasses	6	lbs
Corn Syrup	10	lbs
Jams	10	lbs
Fruit drink powdered	24	lbs
Flavored Gelatin	6	lbs
Total Sugars	236	lbs

Fats and Oils		
Shortening	16	lbs
Vegetable Oil	8	gal
Mayonnaise	8	qts
Salad Dressing	6	qts
Peanut Butter	16	lbs
Total Fats	54	lbs

Milk		
Dry Milk	240	lbs
Evaporated Milk	48	can
Other	50	lbs
Total Dairy	298	lbs

Legumes		
Beans, dry	120	lbs
Lima Beans	14	lbs
Soy Beans	40	lbs
Split Peas	14	lbs
Lentils	14	lbs
Dry Soup Mix	14	lbs
Total Legumes	216	lbs

Cooking Essentials		
Baking Powder	6	lbs
Baking Soda	6	lbs
Yeast	3	lbs
Salt	22	lbs
Vinegar	3	gal

Water		
Water	84	gal

1. Collect homesteading materials. Whether you stay home, camp in your yard, or live in the mountains, it will all be useful. We will also gather together to share, don't stress over not having everything. Food should be your primary concern. The ability to grow, harvest, store and cook. Work on that first.

2. Collect warm clothing, blankets and shoes, no matter what size it is. There will be no electricity for years and fuel sources will be limited. Stores will not be available. You will be helping many others who arrive with nothing. Tell others you are collecting and you will receive a good supply.

3. Be calamity ready. Store in the trunk of a car (parked outside of the garage) gloves, shoes, coats, flashlights, water and food. Bury extra keys away from the house.

4. Have a family council. Have a meet up spot for rescuing. Maps of the area, phone lists, I.D. for children (in case you don't make it) and 2-way radios in faraday bags for communicating.

5. Store up for easy loading and getting away. There is a buckets and bins list on the website to help you. Most families already have these items in their homes. Organize it!

Prepping Ideas to Consider

Fuel Sources

Whole house natural gas generator. When electricity or gas is shut off, switch over to run it on propane.

Wood is a natural source, but if every one in the state is looking for wood it becomes scarce. It also takes 6 months to cure before it will burn.

Propane. Converters can be put on fireplaces, stoves, hot water heaters, etc., to run on propane. It can be stored long term. It cannot be "turned off" by the government/utility companies.

Gasoline generators are great for temporary emergencies and are dependant on availability of gasoline.

Off grid electricity resources:

➤Portable, EMP proof
➤Runs small refrigerator, crock pot, lights, Coleman Hot Water unit, freezer.
➤Cons: Will not run a small heater, power tools, etc. Cost is $3k

➤Runs laptop, phone and Ipods (pics/games/music), electric toothbrush
➤Approximately $100

➤Inexpensive to use a flashlights and room lights. No need for batteries.

Cooking Sources

Tripod for campfire cooking. Large stock pots and rod iron pots and pans will be needed.

Temporary propane camp grill. Limited to availability of propane.

Sun Oven is free energy, but is limited to the cloudy skies.

Coleman Hot Water on Demand – within 4 seconds converts cold water to 100 degrees. Runs on battery (44 gallons to a charge). Use solar to charge.

Additional Kitchen tools will help in preparing meals.

Shelter Sources

Alaknak or deep winter tents with a tent stove is probably the most economical. Bring smaller tents to put inside to create zone within a zone (less heat needed).

Canvas army tents are durable and warm but extremely heavy if you have to carry it.

Excellent for yard camping.

Geo and Turtle tents allow for hammocks inside, 8 feet of snow on top, and insulation panels. The price is $3k+

Tent trailers bumper pulls RV's are all excellent if you can get them into deep wooded areas.

Food Supplies
Fast and Furious Food Storage

Need: Long term, with and without electricity and emergency.

What to do with old, out dated food: Red Herring Room/Second location (give to robbers). Dreamers say old food is "blessed".

Church guidelines: only 1 cup beans, 1 small loaf of bread per day.

Collect as much nutrient dense (grains and proteins) food you can (wheat, rice, oats, spelt, beans, etc.) Freeze-dried foods are "processed" and expensive. Only use them for hard to get items (meats/cheeses/dairy). Only 10% of the church has a one year or more supply. Wheat will make a great barter commodity and is cheap now!

We will grow the fresh stuff – SPROUTING from your seeds/grains !! 400% more protein than meat, available in 24-72 hours.

We will hunt and homestead meat and eggs.

Water Supplies

Berkey is rated #1 and filters out just about everything. Starts at $200 This is an essential item for drinking water in the mountains.

PUR is the #1 rated home system. No need to buy an expensive unit, this one works. Stock up on filters.

Water storage is essential for short term and long term. Proper bottles make a difference. Some water needs to be portable.

During a crisis, water can be off for weeks. A 250 gallon tank would be essential to survival. $250 Collect rain/snow water with buckets and store in larger tanks.

Sanitation Supplies

Line toilets at home if the water goes off.

The best way to stop disease in camp is to have a bucket for each person.

Each page of phone books makes a great piece of toilet paper.

Peri-bottles or squirt bottles will "wash" and then you can "dry" (before toilet paper was invented).

21853919R00071

Made in the USA
San Bernardino, CA
10 June 2015